Oksana Shapoval

Wagner's concept of Kunstreligion through the prism of the mystery beginning

AF301544

Oksana Shapoval

Wagner's concept of Kunstreligion through the prism of the mystery beginning

monographic study

ScienciaScripts

Imprint

Any brand names and product names mentioned in this book are subject to trademark, brand or patent protection and are trademarks or registered trademarks of their respective holders. The use of brand names, product names, common names, trade names, product descriptions etc. even without a particular marking in this work is in no way to be construed to mean that such names may be regarded as unrestricted in respect of trademark and brand protection legislation and could thus be used by anyone.

Cover image: www.ingimage.com

This book is a translation from the original published under ISBN 978-620-2-01478-6.

Publisher:
Sciencia Scripts
is a trademark of
Dodo Books Indian Ocean Ltd. and OmniScriptum S.R.L publishing group

120 High Road, East Finchley, London, N2 9ED, United Kingdom
Str. Armeneasca 28/1, office 1, Chisinau MD-2012, Republic of Moldova, Europe
Printed at: see last page
ISBN: 978-620-7-69550-8

CONTENTS.

1

From the author

Wagner's text has a concentrated content, encouraging interpreters/recipients to endlessly explore it, to find its deepest meanings. The composer addresses cultural experience, bringing encrypted codes into his works. In the process of creativity there is a "communicative act" (according to Y. Lotman [24, p. 11]), in which in the process of R. Wagner's formation of a unique picture of the world there is a qualitative reinterpretation of generally significant symbols. At the same time, according to the Kun- streligion concept, art seemed to R. Wagner to be equal to religion in its significance. "Parsifal" is a drama-mystery crowning the composer's creative path. However, all his opera works, beginning with The Flying Dutchman, are approaches to the formation of the idea of Kunstreligion and the writing of a solemn stage mystery in three acts that crowns his creative path. Thus, the mystery beginning is characteristic of R. Wagner's work as a whole.

The composer dreamed of building a theater and organizing festivals where his operas would be performed exclusively. The realization of Wagner's plans and the staging of his works can be likened to the sacrament of initiation - the initiation into the supreme Truth, which the composer communicated on the pages of his musical and aesthetic works and then embodied in majestic creations of the spirit - grandiose musical and stage canvases. In accordance with the composer's idea of Kunstreligion, the Festspielhaus is a temple of art. It is situated, like many religious buildings, on a hill surrounded by a delightful park. A stage performance at the Festspielhaus can rightly be characterized as a sacred act in a temple of art.

Wagner's text, in accordance with its content and the depth of the author's concept, is on a par with the great monuments of the human spirit represented not only in the sphere of art, but also in such forms of social consciousness as religion and philosophy.

Wagner's text, in accordance with its content and depth of the author's concept, is on a par with the great monuments of the human spirit, represented not only in the sphere of art, but also in such forms of social consciousness as religion and philosophy. And this is not accidental, as Wagner in his cognitive activity gravitated towards sources where a generalized picture of the world was reflected.

The cognitive sphere of R. Wagner. Wagner's cognitive sphere, his thesaurus can be likened to a space within which "the realization of communicative processes and the development of new information is possible" [24, p.]. [24, c. 11]. The characteristic given by Yu. Lotman's characterization of the semiosphere is consistent with the nature of meaning-forming constants of the "hermetic" space of Wagner's myth-making, the "breeding ground" of which were the universally significant codes of world culture. According to R. Barthes, the text is not identical to the work. Not only the author, but also the text itself "speaks" to the recipient through the work [3, p. 416]. Thus, the interpreter enters into a virtual dialog not only with the creator of the work, but also with the text itself. The identification of the semantic content of compositions, including by interpreter-researchers, invariably proves the potentially infinite multiplicity of possible interpretations. The depth of interpretation depends on the conceptual content of the text of the work, on the one hand, and on the thesaurus of the recipient, peculiarities of his thinking, professional attitudes and skills, on the other.

The author of the book aims to interpret the work of R. Wagner through the prism of mystery, which is reflected in the idea of immortality, angelic service and redemption.

Mystery and Mysterium in the works of R. Wagner

The mystery path of self-discovery in "Parsifal" is described in the dissertation study by E. Naumova [30]. Naumova [30]. The author sees in this work the concentration of the fundamental properties of mystery. However, the mystery beginning is refracted in Wagner's work in another sense, for example, as an aesthetic action aimed at purification, sanctification of the degraded society. For R. Wagner, the theater is a temple of art, so his dream of freeing the musical theater from the ways of commercialization echoes the Gospel story of Jesus expelling merchants from the temple.

An expansive understanding of mystery in Wagner's works arises due to the use of literary analogies. B. Shalaginov called the tragedy "Faust" a mystery. The correlation of Goethe's work with Dante's "Divine Comedy" (following Schelling's hint) prompts B. Shalaginov to borrow the names of the parts of the great Italian's work to designate the main milestones of Faust's formation and spiritual discipleship - hell, purgatory and paradise. The researcher measures mystery in "Faust" by the three-member history, which starts from the conscious break of man with the "sinful", low past through a meaningful choice in the present to the ascension of the soul, the epiphany of "new life" in the future [40, p. 12].

Wagner also made an inner ascent to the Absolute, immersing himself in the artistic world of Dante's Divine Comedy. In a letter to Liszt of June 7, 1855, the composer wrote about it: "I was climbing from one step to another, killing one passion after another. I was overcoming a wild thirst for life. But now, having reached the last flame, having defeated the very will to live, I threw myself into the fire to completely melt in the contemplation of Beatrice, to finally disembodied my personality" [12, p. 110]. [12, c. 110].

Ф. W. Schelling in his unfinished work "Philosophy of Art" correlates "The Divine Comedy" with the tragedy "Faust". Doctor of Philosophy A. Gulyga in his monographic work "Schelling" addresses to the thoughts of the German philosopher concerning the parallel between the mentioned literary works. Thus, Schelling saw the essence of the genre of comedy in the transfer of necessity from the object to the subject. When a coward is forced to be brave, when a miser has to squander his wealth, the wife plays the role of the husband and vice versa. In such cases there is a comic effect. Schelling called Goethe's comedy "Faust" the greatest poetic work of the German people [cited in: 15, p. 43]. According to Schelling, Faust wastes his potentialities: "What Mephistopheles predicted is realized:

I will give him life in abundance,

I'll trample it in the mud, I'll bury it in mud.

I'll have him go through all the horror, all the torture,

All the filth of nothingness, all the emptiness!" (translated by B. Pasternak).

A. Gulyba also points out: "In these words of Mephistopheles, which Schelling quotes, in his opinion, concluded the meaning of the poem. The second part of "Faust", full of tragic pathos, where the hero gains freedom and acts as a moral person, at that time had not yet been written" [ibid].

In Wagner's operas, similarly to Dante's Divine Comedy and Goethe's Faust, there is also a mysterious three-part plot, as the inner fall of the hero-sinner is replaced by a spiritual turning point leading to redemption. "Death in Love" (Liebestod) in R. Wagner's mystery has a meaning close to the wisdom of mystery: "Everything to which a man is attached in ordinary life must at the end of the spiritual journey of the mystic lose all meaning for him. The true value for him now is love" [41].

P. R. Steiner connects inner becoming and transformation with the acquisition of spiritual vision: "Now man looks inside himself. As a hidden creative force, still deprived of being, the divine beats in his soul. This is the area where the enchanted god can come to life again" [ibid]. By the same reflections are put into the mouth of Jesus in Wagner's unfinished drama "Jesus of Nazareth": "And now I want to return man to man, teaching him again to seek God in himself, and no longer outside himself; but God is the law of love; and when we realize this and act according to this law as every creature unconsciously acts, we will be God himself, for God is the realization of himself" [21, p. 170]. [21, c. 170]. In the opera Lohengrin, Elsa discovers the divine through an inner gaze turned to herself. It is not by chance that as long as the heroine remained true to her inner vision, she followed the will of her heart. Having turned her gaze outward, the heroine was deprived of the innermost divine beginning, which revealed itself to her in a moment of danger and called for the help of the Grail knight. In this connection, let us recall Fr. G. Florovsky's judgment about the two cultures - night and day. It is in the opposition of intuitive and logical beginnings that the tragedy of Elsa's character lies, who, possessing intuitive purity and faith (nocturnal, subconscious culture), could not withstand the trials leading her to the Light (day culture), deny the arguments of logical proof (spiritual sickness) and make a conscious choice in favor of love. Thus, the heroine does not reach the ultimate goal of mystery formation. Characteristically, the ultimate Truth is revealed to Elsa through a dream, which is akin to a mystical vision. E. Schüré writes in his book "The Great Initiates": "The mystical chronicles of all times show that spiritual truths of the highest order were cognized by the chosen souls not by means of speculation, but by means of inner contemplation under the form of vision. This kind of psychic phenomena is very little known to modern science, but they represent an undoubted fact" [42]. C. G. Jung cites a number of documented cases when deeply believing, religiously inclined mystics had visions of symbols (trinity, the face of God's wrath), which the psychologist considers as archetypes of the collective unconscious [43, p. 101 - 104].

According to E. Schüré, Jesus contemplated the "supreme truth of his own inner world" and it illuminated his spirit with the power of love and gave him spiritual fortitude: "This sense of union with God in the light of Love was Jesus' first great revelation. It illuminated his whole life and gave him unshakable confidence. It made Him meek and irresistible, it made of His thought a shining shield, of His word a fiery sword." [42]. A deep esoteric meaning is contained in the fate of Lohengrin. "'For the soul descending from heaven, birth is death,' said Empedocles 500 years before Christ'" [ibid]. The inner essence of Lohengrin is opposite to the laws of the world into which he descended. In this contradiction lies the tragedy of his personality.

Absolute Love as the initiating intention and goal (accession to it through sacrifice, cognition of it as an unconditional ontological value in the light of truthfulness) of the path of self-discovery in Wagner's operas corresponds with the Christian mystery, one of the basic commandments of which is "love thy neighbor". The heroes of Wagner lead the sinner to purification and renewal in the transcendent world - the meaning of Liebestod.

In connection with the above, it can be argued that the mystery beginning defines the essential basis of R. Wagner's artistic consciousness.

Formation of the idea of immortality in R. Wagner's artistic reflection

The author of the monograph touches upon the worldview problems of R. Wagner's artistic creation through the prism of his continuous dialog with the cultural and historical heritage. The focus of attention is on the mechanisms of realization in the composer's artistic consciousness of the metaphysical idea of immortality, which is associated with semantic synthesis. It conjugates various heuristic sources of R. Wagner, generalizing the spiritual and cognitive experience of mankind.

The artistic consciousness of the Bayreuth master is a unique and multidimensional cultural and historical phenomenon. We turn to the thesaurus of R. Wagner. Wagner's thesaurus, which was directly embodied in his reflection and creativity, one can find the refraction of the idea of immortality through the prism of ancient tragedy and philosophy, Christian and Buddhist ideas, Schopenhauerian ethics, while the reader's horizons signal the diversity of his knowledge. Wagner's direct interest in the problem of the dialectics of death and immortality is indicated by his familiarization with the philosophical treatise by L. Feuerbach, where both concepts are key ("Thoughts on Death and Immortality"). Close to the composer was "the idea that only a sublime act and spiritualized work of art is truly immortal" [11, p. 129]. [11, c. 129].

The idea of immortality as a meaning image in the work of R. Wagner is connected with his cognitive processes. In this regard, it is necessary to present the contextual field of this idea through the prism of cultural and historical experience and its projection in the artistic consciousness and creativity of the composer. It is also necessary to take into account that in the context of the formation of R. Wagner's worldview and his creative aspirations the idea of immortality was not a "constant value", because in the process of the composer's inner formation its comprehension deepened.

P. Wagner synthesized various sources, finding common ground in them, discovering ideas akin to his own spiritual quest. In a letter to A. Reckel dated February 5, 1855, the composer formulates the essence of his own personal dialogue with A.

Schopenhauer: "I will say frankly that in my own life experience I have come to the point where only his philosophy can satisfy me and determine the course of my thoughts. By the fact that I have unhesitatingly accepted all his very, very serious truths, I have resolutely gone to meet the deepest demands of my own self." And although Schopenhauer led my thought on a new road, different from the previous one, it must be said that all this fascination with him is quite consistent with *the* inherent *suffering* in me, *harmonizing with the suffering of the world* " [italics mine - O. Sh.] [12, p. 192]. In the diary entries of R. Wagner (October 1, 1858) we find the composer's reflections on the ideas of suffering and compassion, love, joy and co-joy interconnected in his consciousness. He sees the true cause of his torment in the impossibility for him to completely detach himself from life and the aspirations of earthly existence. At the same time, R. Wagner is frightened by the very focus on achieving material prosperity, because the rich, in his opinion, cannot be called truly happy people, but their behavior and outlook is contented, which repels the composer from their way of life completely. He is more sympathetic to the poorer classes of society, arousing compassion in his soul. Compassion itself, as the composer emphasizes, is not conditioned by "the individual characteristics of the suffering person" [12, p. 246]. [12, c. 246]. Love, on the contrary, allows a person to rise "to co-joy, and we share the joy of a person only if his individual characteristics are extremely pleasant and related to us" [ibid.]. [ibid.] Here he also writes about high nature, which is close to his own aspirations: "A high nature is what it is, precisely because through its own suffering it has risen to self-denial, or because it retains and develops in itself the inclination to such a feat. It is directly close to me, equal, and with such a nature I can have a common co-joy" [12, c. 248]. And this sense of co-joy is spilled in Wagner's Liebestod, filled with the greatest self-denial and spiritual peace at the same time, reflected in the perception of the recipient who grasps the meaning of the operatic opuses of the Bayreuth genius.

Turning to the composer's reflection, we can conclude that the metaphysical idea of immortality is directly connected in his consciousness with the overcoming of suffering through intense confrontation with higher forces, death, leading to the highest stage of inner self-knowledge. At various periods of his artistic development, the composer drew such ideas from a variety of mythological, religious, legendary and artistic sources. The unity of spiritual and physical suffering is revealed in the images of Wagner's heroes Tristan and Amfortas. It is no accident that these characters are conceptualized by the composer in a single contextual key. Evidence of this can be found in his memoirs, where the composer recalls the process of creating the libretto of Tristan: "In the last act I included an episode which, however, I did not use: in search of the Grail, Tristan is visited by Parsifal. Suffering from a wound, ready to die Tristan is identified in my sketch with Amfortas from the romantic narrative about the Grail" [11, p. 246]. [11, c. 246]. Both characters experience acute disharmony, pain, a sense of unfreedom, conflict between reality and what their inner self is striving for, but their torment is a necessary condition for ascending and finding peace - the much-desired harmony, spiritual peace, hard-won liberation from the tragic collisions of existence.

Such meanings are deeply rooted in the cultural and historical experience of mankind, because suffering forms a whole with the life process itself. In Buddhism, the wheel of samsara, which draws nature and humankind into its endless run, is a symbol uniting these beginnings. Life and suffering are inextricably linked to the comprehension of the world, spiritual perfection and self-knowledge. Let us recall, for example, the biblical two-valued tree of life and knowledge, tasting the fruits of which man commits the fall into sin and experiences a heavy fate of suffering. Thus, sinfulness and torments of earthly existence appear in the Old Testament in the context of cause-and-effect relations, forming a semantic chain: knowledge → sin → suffering. The perception of the ontological process from the perspective of the sinful fall is determined by the polar opposition of light and darkness, the absolutization of good and evil.

Wagner turned to Buddhist doctrine in the mature period of his creative work, comprehending the idea of self-denial inherent in it in the opera Tristan und Isolde, the tetralogy The Ring of the Nibelung, the mystery Parsifal and the dramatic poem

The Victorious. However, one cannot speak of unconditional adherence to a certain philosophical or religious doctrine, since the composer's artistic consciousness is characterized by the accumulation of multidimensional information through the prism of a distinctive, original and independent in its development worldview: various sources pushed the composer's thought and contributed to the deepening of the constant archetypes of creativity that had developed in the 40s. For example, Parsifal, Wagner's last work, is closely connected not only with Christian mystery, but also with the Buddhist worldview: along with the semantics of bell ringing, chorale and the Eucharist, the Buddhist idea of compassion for all living beings is evident, the image of the swan is interpreted as a sacred animal; overcoming sensuality is associated with Christian chastity and Buddhist nirvana.

The meaning of suffering, however, is also found in the bright Hellenistic worldview, seemingly far from Buddhist and Christian asceticism. Fate and doom, which naturally entail a fierce struggle, torment and death, determine the originality of the mythological picture of the world; submission to the fate, the impossibility of overcoming the world's destiny determine the tragedy of the worldview of the epoch. An example of a mythological hero is Wotan, who feels the inseparability of his own suffering with the fate of the world; the personal drama of the anthropomorphic deity resonates with the world's sorrow; thanks to spiritual torments, which activate his inner search, he rises to higher and higher stages of self-knowledge.

A vivid example of comprehension of the tragedy of existence, which is conditioned by the realization of its imperfection, can serve as Socrates' deathbed dialogue presented by Plato. In the dialog "Phaedon", Socrates, facing death, reveals the higher meaning of existence, which lies not in the material-death, but in the spiritual existence of man. The philosopher discusses the pleasant and the painful, the impossibility of suicide, since man, being subject to the will of the gods, has no moral right to deprive himself of life[1] , he reflects on his own aspiration to a posthumous,

---

1 Buddhists have a different attitude to suicide. The goal in this religious and philosophical doctrine is to stop the endless series of rebirths. If a person kills himself, then in the next life he will have to find himself in a similar situation, everything will be repeated again, so suicide is senseless. In order to end suffering, one

more perfect existence, on spiritual healing, which comes at the moment of transition to the next world. In many ways, the ancient Greek philosopher anticipates the Christian worldview, but spirituality, which he conceives as something far above the transient, mortal, still has a different meaning, devoid of Christian antagonism to the sensual world. In Plato, inner rebirth is associated with the birth of immortal essence in the human soul "I", which is possible due to thinking and creation as manifestations of the highest in man due to those spiritual potencies that contribute to deep cognition and self-knowledge, mutual enrichment in the process of interpersonal communication.

A rich inner life, full of joys and torments, enriches the human being: in this regard, let us recall R. Wagner's reflections on the high nature, which he thinks of as equal to himself. This idea is fully applicable to Plato's dialogue "Phaedon", but to the greatest extent it corresponds to the spirit of ancient Greek tragedies, which served as a prototype for Wagner of the art of the future. Driven by fate through struggle and torment, the tragic hero, striving for a noble goal, perishes in the strain of all his inner strength, arousing the audience's deepest compassion. Euripides, Virgil, Sophocles, Aeschylus and Homer revealed to Wagner the charms of the Hellenistic worldview; Shakespeare, Goethe and Schiller revealed to the composer the further ways in which the theatrical art was being developed in the aspect of the continuation of classical traditions. Let us turn to R. Wagner's reflections in his work "The Work of Future Art", where the composer discusses the meaning of the death of a character as the logical conclusion of the collisions of an artistic work: "For dramatic art, the most appropriate and most worthy subject of representation seems to be such an action, which ends simultaneously with the life of the protagonist, which receives its true conclusion with the completion of the life of this person" [8, p. 249]. [8, c. 249]. The German composer reveals the reasons for and necessity of such an end in a musical drama: the protagonist "<...> convinces us irrefutably only when he really perishes in the exertion of all his forces, when his personal drama is subordinated to the necessity of his being; when he proves to us the truth of his being not only by his

____

must follow the principles commanded by the Buddha (the eightfold path).

actions - they may seem arbitrary to us while he is acting - but also by sacrificing his personality" [ibid.]. [ibid.]

From ancient times, torment has been thought not only as a sad fate, but also as a natural test on the path of spiritual ascent, inner self-improvement. We find a similar situation in the work of R. Wagner, starting with the operas of the 40s: the mental anguish of the Flying Dutchman, Tannhäuser, and later Tristan, Wotan, Kundry, Parsifal serve as a catalyst for their inner search leading to redemption. This mythologeme is conditioned by the deep prerequisites of cultural and historical experience: ancient Greek tragedy and various branches of religious consciousness reflect the anciently realized connection between spiritual quest and the true existence of man; inner dissatisfaction is closely connected with the antinomies of freedom and necessity, immortality and the end of life. In the dramaturgy of Wagner's operas, death is interpreted not as the inevitable destruction of the physical shell, but as "life beyond the grave", signifying redemption and deliverance, overcoming the tragedy of existence, enlightenment and the posthumous ascension of the spirit.

Let us also recall R. Wagner's reflections that the rich repel him with their contentment and he is closer to the high nature inclined to self-denial. In this connection, an analogy with the Christian worldview arises. The famous saying: "It is easier for a camel to go through the eye of a needle than for a rich man to enter the kingdom of heaven" comes to mind. According to the Indian legend, Buddha was a royal son who received an excellent education, but at the age of 29 left the palace to go on a long journey. The purpose of this journey was cognition and self-discovery. In R. Wagner's work we meet many characters who accomplish the path of knowledge in the physical and metaphysical sense: the Flying Dutchman, Tannhäuser, Siegfried, Wotan, Parsifal.

The peculiarity of R. Wagner's interpretation of the idea of redemption (which in Christianity was thought of as a guarantee of paradise eternal life) is that he correlated it not only with sacrificial love and spiritual search, but also with allegory.

The peculiarity of Wagner's interpretation of the idea of redemption (which in Christianity was thought of as a guarantee of paradise eternal life) lies in the fact that he correlated it not only with sacrificial love and spiritual quest, but also with the allegorical figure of the goddess of Revolution, who marks the fall of the old world and the birth of a new one from its wreckage: "She comes on the wings of the storm with a high raised forehead, illuminated by the brilliance of lightning, with a sword in her right hand and a torch in her left hand, with gloomy, cold and punishing eyes, but with eyes that radiate the radiance of the purest love for those who dare to look point-blank into these dark eyes" [9, p. 41] [9, c. 41]. P. Wagner dreamed of social reorganization, universal prosperity, but, first of all, in his mind imprinted the image of the ideal revolution, which is designed, pointing to the era of universal equality, to create a "paradise on earth" and at the same time a new union of arts, the phenomenon of the perfect work of art of the future. At the head of this movement he sees Christ and Apollo. Although the composer's attitude to Christianity was not as unambiguous as to the beauty of antiquity, as we can judge from the pamphlet "Art and Revolution", it is the Christian Messiah that he interprets as the herald of world brotherhood based on a deep moral foundation. Summarizing his reflections on the theme of revolution (reformation) in art, he writes: "So, Christ has shown us that we, men, are all equal and brothers; Apollo has stamped this great fraternal association with power and beauty and has guided man, doubting his dignity, to the consciousness of his highest divine power" [8, p. 141]. [8, c. 141]. The composer's ideas about social transformation, the realization of which R. Wagner in the late 40s thought as a revolution leading to a new era of love and mutual understanding, allows us to complete the semantic chain, presenting it as a certain analog of the world apocalypse, when the grains will be separated from the chaff. At the same time, in Christianity, the advent of higher justice will be preceded by a terrible picture of the destruction and collapse of the sinful world, which will culminate in the triumph of eternal life in its paradisiacal understanding (according to the Revelation of St. John the Theologian).

In connection with the idea of revolution, we should mention the factor of the intersection of R. Wagner's name and Russian culture. Significant biographical facts include the composer's acquaintance with Mikhail Bakunin and their communication, which in many ways served as an impetus for Wagner's reflections. As a great artist-reformer, Wagner dreamed of reorganizing art and establishing a commune - a community of creative individuals, which would contribute to the growth of the spiritual potential of his fellow citizens (the composer's socio-aesthetic utopia). There are also other points of contact between the two cultures, associated with certain figurative parallels with Russian literature. The understanding of revolution as an apocalyptic redemption that transforms and renews the world at the cost of the collapse of the old social order, when bloodshed, death and destruction are inevitable, unites the work of R. Wagner with A. Blok's poem "The Twelve". It is indicative that the very title of the work appeals to Christian numerical symbolism. In the Revelation of John the Theologian the heavenly Jerusalem is described as follows: it "has a great and high wall, has twelve gates and on them twelve angels, on the gates are written the names of the twelve tribes of the children of Israel: from the east three gates, from the north three gates, from the south three gates, from the west three gates; the wall of the city has twelve foundations, and on them are the names of the twelve apostles and of the Lamb" [Revelation 21: 12 - 12 - the Lamb]. [Rev. 21: 12 - 14]. In his poetic revelation (this is how we can characterize the work of the Russian poet from the perspective of Christian eschatology), A. Blok sees a fascinating and at the same time frightening picture of the revolution, at the head of which he sees Christ "with a white crown of roses" and the twelve apostles. Here there are obvious parallels with R. Wagner. It is not by chance that A. Blok calls Wagner's grandiose opera cycle "social tetralogy" [cited in: 23, 23, 23]. [quoted in: 23, p. 113], capturing in it the spirit of the era, thinking it part of the political views of the German composer, which he expressed in the work "Art and Revolution". Thus, Wagner the revolutionary was close to Blok the artist with his social-Christian views.

The tragedy of supreme power, the "loneliness of the leader", and, moreover, the reformer, whose ideas were not to the liking of many, are shown in V. Merezhkovsky's novel Julian the Apostate. The good motives of the head of the

Roman power, seeking to revive the former greatness of the state, collides with historical realities, which leads to the formation of a spiritual gap between the ruler and the people. There is also a misunderstanding with the immediate environment, which previously supported him. The Russian writer focuses on the ideas of counter-revolution, political conspiracy, the volatility of political sentiment and popular commitment. V. Merezhkovsky reflects on the charm of the Hellenistic worldview, which was irretrievably lost, on Christian spiritualism and asceticism, intolerance of Christians to other religions and eroticism. At the same time, he shows the points of contact between the two eras, revealing the duality of Julian's own soul. All these circumstances allow us to put this novel on a par with the spiritual quest of R. Wagner, who was constantly concerned with similar themes. Let us remember the title character of the opera "Rienzi", his desire to revive the former greatness of Rome and bitter loneliness, when the only loyal companion was his sister Irena. On the other hand, there is Tannhäuser's tossing between the vector-different tendencies of sensual and spiritual life, which symbolize the two poles in the hero's soul, actualized through an appeal to archetypal images such as the Roman goddess of sensual love and beauty Venus and the immaculate Virgin Mary. The composer's reflection records his constant meditations on the dialectic of Christianity and paganism and his own deeply personal understanding of this theme. P. Wagner invariably juxtaposes and contrasts these two eras in human history, often not in favor of Christianity, in which he sees the preconditions of human hypocrisy. The mystery of Julian the Apostate's path is connected with the loss of spiritual reference points, because while dreaming of the revival of paganism, he is not completely free from Christian ideals, which causes irreconcilable contradictions in his soul. Wagner, on the contrary, reflects on the theme of the religion of the future, which he conceives of as the unification of Christian and Apollonian principles. The composer actualizes this idea in the author's programmatic explanation to the overture to "Tannhäuser", which he concludes with a metaphorical summary: "And both previously separated elements, spirit and sensuality, God and earthly nature, merge in a single sacred kiss of love" [1, p. 58]. [1, c. 58]. I recall that the composer expressed a similar idea in his brochure "Art and Revolution" - the need to transform society in the spirit of uniting Christian and Apollonian principles.

Being a necessary condition for the limitlessness of the human finite, love overcomes everything, even death (this idea is consonant with both antiquity and Christianity). The ancient myth of Orpheus and Eurydice reveals the intense opposition between love and death. However, in the Hellenistic consciousness there is not only a separation, but also a combination of these concepts. In Plato's dialog "The Feast" the idea that man strives for immortality, i.e. continuation of himself in children, pupils, manifestation of spiritual potential in creativity, thanks to which the name of the creator remains in the memory of future generations, is consistently carried out. Such comprehension of the idea of immortality is defined by the ancient Greek philosopher by the concept of Eros, which he thought of as aspiration to truth, perfection, creation.

In addition to the marvelous, according to R. Wagner himself, dialogues of Plato, among which he singles out "The Feast" [11, p. 10], the composer was always concerned with the Gospel motifs. In the Gospel the idea of immortality receives a slightly different refraction in relation to antiquity, although we should not completely distinguish these historical periods and think of them as absolute antitheses. In the Christian consciousness, Love, Death and Eternity are conjugated into a single semantic whole: death does not appear as non-existence, but as otherness, which gives the possibility of transition of the righteous and truly repentant sinners into the sphere of perfect existence. Death is not the end of existence, but only the termination of earthly perishable presence, since it does not cut off the life of the immortal soul. In the Holy Scriptures, Jesus says: "But God is not the God of the dead, but of the living" [Lk. 20: 38], referring to the possibility of eternal existence through the great sacrifice. St. Paul writes: "Christ is risen from the dead, the firstborn from the dead <...> As in Adam all die, so in Christ all will be made alive" [1 Cor. 15: 20; 20]. [1 Cor. 15: 20; 15: 22]. By his death, passing into immortality, he gives redeemed mankind the hope of resurrection, indicating the possibility of eternal paradise life; according to the Easter hymn, "Christ is risen from the dead, having put death to death and given life to those who are in the tombs!".

The Christian Messiah is a symbol of morality, who revealed the turning point of universal moral and ethical norms: it is not by chance that there is a division of world history - before and after the birth of Christ. The significance of sacred events in the formation of humanity's self-consciousness is undeniable. Suffering and Love form an inseparable whole in the Christian mystery; the sufferings of Jesus on the cross are inseparably connected with the boundless Love of God, being a testimony of the supreme Fatherly Mercy for all redeemed mankind and a sign of imperishable spiritual Truth. The sufferings of Christ, who appears in Scripture as an innocent victim, make it possible to believe in eternity, to overcome death, to attain immortality, because the Lamb of God took upon himself all the sins of mankind, beginning with the fall of Adam.

Christianity seems to be illuminated from within by the emotion of compassion. The idea of empathy is found as early as in ancient Greek tragedies: catharsis is born as a result of empathy with the hero, whose fate evokes an active emotional response in the audience. Compassion is the opposite of selfishness. In this regard, Schopenhauer's philosophical ethics can be presented as a link that unites ancient tragedy, Christianity and Buddhism. The German philosopher believed that all true and pure love, agape, catharsis is always compassion. Eros as another facet of love is interpreted by him as selfishness, self-love. Through the prism of Schopenhauer's doctrine, the worldview axis of R. Wagner's artistic consciousness is outlined, which lies in the idea of death and immortality.

Eros and Agape appear as two types of love, both within the psychology of the individual and as a symbol of the world cosmogony, the highest mercy. In ancient tragedy, catharsis is compassion, purification, release from unhealthy mental movements, and emotional release through contemplation of universally significant phenomena. The spectator rises above individual feelings and motivations to the level of affects that are universal in their significance. Christianity is associated with mercy, Agape, sobornost, active empathy. Compassion is inherent in Buddhism, but here it has a different, more passive character, expressed in the non-attribution of evil. Schopenhauer's denial of the will to life is in harmony with the Buddhist nirvana, which is considered in this doctrine as the summit of moral self-knowledge, and to a certain extent it echoes Christian monastic asceticism.

Empathy is an uplifting feeling associated with the inner, spiritual and soulful world. In this regard, let us recall the images of Senta and Elisabeth, who were imbued with the anguish of a suffering sinner. Tannhäuser embarked on the path of redemption through sympathy with the maiden angel, who shed tears of heartache and despair, and achieved liberation from sin as a result of the shock (inconceivable without empathy) when he met the funeral procession with the body of Elizabeth. In the most generalized form, the idea of compassion is presented in the drama-mystery that crowns the creative path of R. Wagner. Parsifal suddenly felt empathy for Amfortas, which prevented him from succumbing to temptation (a moment of spiritual insight).

Mercy is the highest capacity of man, which finds absolute expression in Christianity. Buddhism lacks an understanding of active empathy. The image of Christ is associated with the deepest pain (mental and bodily) and arouses compassion through the details that make up the mystery of the four Gospels. How human is the anguish of Jesus, who begs the Lord to let this cup pass him by, and yet is ready to drink it to the bottom if it is the will of the heavenly Father. He experienced the bitterness of betrayal and mockery, and being tormented by the pains of the cross, He cried out: "My God, My God, why have You forsaken Me?" [Mk. 15: 34].

The image of the suffering Savior was close to the spiritual quest of R. Wagner, who thought compassion was the highest manifestation of morality and human nature. The Christian idea permeates the composer's entire creative legacy. The sacral image of Christ is directly refracted in the sketches for the drama Jesus of Nazareth; in the drama-mystery Parsifal his holy face is captured this time in the minds of the Grail knights - martyred, sacrificial, bringing redemption and deliverance. The image of Christ is reflected in Kundry's memory, awakening in her soul the anguish of conscience and the longing to free herself from the chains of voluptuousness.

The roots of the meaning of the image of compassion in Wagner's work (in its Christian refraction) should be sought in the composer's childhood experiences, on whom evangelical ideas had a profound effect. The Bayreuth master carried his careful attitude to sacred images and rituals through his entire life right up to the creation of the mystery drama that crowned his creative career. Recalling the Eucharist, a rite that took place on Easter 1827, the composer writes in his memoirs that by that time he, who had recently been gazing with painful passion at the altar image in church and dreaming in prayerful ecstasy of taking the place of the Savior on the cross, had lost such a reverent respect for the authority of the church. However, something completely different was happening in the depths of his soul during the church sacrament itself: *"<..> the* act of distributing holy communion began, the choirs began to sing, the organ rang, and we all, the confirmands, moved in procession around the altar. The thrill that seized me at the rite of the Eucharist was so deeply imprinted in my memory that, fearing in the future not to find in myself such a mood, I never went to communion again" [10, p. 56]. [10, c. 56].

The holy face of Jesus in the sketches for the drama and the ideas carried by the redeeming heroes Senta, Elisabeth, Brünnhilde and Parsifal are a natural embodiment of an internal, inherently personal dialog with Gospel motifs within the framework of the composer's myth-making. The regularity of such a judgment is based on the fact that the composer himself thought of generally significant religious symbols within the framework of art - "art as a 'signifying game' frees these symbols from their dogmatic seriousness" (Wagner's conversation with Cosima of April 28, 1880, recorded in the diaries of the composer's wife) [quoted in: 45, p. 22].

Religious consciousness is associated with the notion of existence beyond the earthly world; it is the essential foundation of the worldview of Christianity and Buddhism. Throughout his creative evolution, Wagner dreamed of the spiritual rebirth of mankind, conceived as a transcendence of sensual reality. The ideal for him was the sacrificial deed of Christ and the self-denial of the benefits of earthly existence of the holy ascetic Buddha, aspiring to nirvana. The religious consciousness of Christianity and Buddhism is defined by spirituality, rejection of the illusions of mortal existence.

Buddha (Sanskrit "bodhi") translates as awakening from the sleep of ignorance. In Tibetan, Buddha sounds like "sang gye." "Sang" means fully purified or awakened and "gye" means open [6]. The cognition of Wagner's Parsifal can also be characterized as an awakening from the sleep of ignorance, liberation from the shackles of ignorance, which has a number of stages: the murder of the swan, repentance, initiation into the sacrament of the Eucharist, mental anguish at the news of the death of his abandoned mother, sensual and bodily temptation, empathy with Amfortas and self-denial, asceticism, holiness.

The belief in the afterlife existed in the pre-Christian period, but it is Christianity that fully raises the problem of moral behavior as a criterion for the postmortem fate of the soul. The idea of death and resurrection can be found in antiquity. Thus, in Euripides' tragedy "Alkesta" the heroine's sacrificial love overcomes death, because even Admet's parents refused to go to the grave for him. Plato cites this act as an example, saying that only those who love each other are ready to die for each other, their devotion to each other can be stronger than the love of blood relatives. The ancient Greek philosopher sees a deep moral underpinning in this act:

"<..> this feat of hers was approved not only by people, but also by the gods, and if of the many mortals who performed beautiful deeds, the gods gave only a few of them the honorable right to return the soul from Hades, then they let her soul out of there, admiring her deed" [31, p. 127]. Related to the idea of healing and resurrection is the figure of the healer Asclepius - the son of the Sun god Apollo, whom Zeus struck with lightning for the resurrection of the dead. The analogy with Christianity in these examples arises through the ideas of luminosity, healing, and overcoming the end of life, pointing to the idea of immortality. Dying Socrates in Plato's dialog "Phaedon", feeling the cold of constraining death, informed those who mourned him about his healing when passing to the next world: "We owe Asclepius a rooster" [31, p. 414]. [31, c. 414]. His saying has a deep meaning - the necessity of sacrifice as a sign of gaining health - the last words of the philosopher, which at first glance contain a paradox, because they have not worldly, typically commonplace, but a mysterious meaning associated with ideas about eternity.

In Egyptian mysteries, the idea of immortality is associated with the cult of Osiris, with the mythological understanding of the cycle of phenomena in nature; this god is the personification of the kingdom of the dead and fertility. The lines of M. Wesendonk's poem "in death the seed of new life" (translated by V. Kolomiytsev), the basis of the song "Mourning" from the vocal cycle "Five Poems by Mathilde Wesendonk" by R. Wagner, come to mind.

According to Egyptian myths, he was a hero and king in Egypt. His cunning brother Seth took his life, but his devoted wife and sister Isis resurrected him. The worship of Osiris is connected with the agricultural cult, in connection with which the ideas of death, resurrection and immortality are conditioned by comprehension of the most important primordial principles of existence. The completion of the cycle is an integral part of the renewal of nature, a manifestation of the eternal periodicity. The milestones of phylogenesis (birth $\rightarrow$ formation $\rightarrow$ extinction $\rightarrow$ death $\rightarrow$ aspiration to new life, continuation of oneself in children) are repeated in each new generation. The analogy between human existence and the ontology of the universe was already noticed in ancient times.

In the archaic consciousness, the ideas of birth, death and rebirth were associated with the daily observed phenomena of sunrise and sunset, which were thought to be united with the cycle of existence, where endlessly changing periods neighbor each other. The figurative and semantic content of the fourth song of R. Wagner's vocal cycle to M. Wesendonk's poems "Sorrow" / "*Schmerzen*" in the unity of poetic and musical components is set by the philosophical interpretation of the archetype: sorrows and joys are realized by the lyrical hero in unity with the solar cycle, natural existence. The morning awakening of nature and the sunset of the heavenly luminary, symbolizing birth and death, are associated with deeply personal experiences, reflections of a suffering, finely feeling person. The lyrical hero is faced with cruel social realities, tragic collisions of existence, but firmly believes that "happiness ripens in a sea of tears" (translated by V. Kolomiitsev).

Along with the constancy of his views, we should note their evolution in the composer's artistic consciousness, who turned to Buddhism in his mature creative period. The nature of his attitude to Buddhist images is evidenced by a biographical fact in the composer's diary. A certain Countess A. sent R. Wagner a small Chinese statuette depicting Buddha. The composer was deeply disgusted by its appearance, which, however, in no way contradicted his reverent attitude to the Buddhist doctrine itself: "How much labor one must put in to protect oneself from such impressions in this all-exhausting world and to preserve pure contemplation of the ideal from all perversions. Those who cannot rise to the level of the ideal and noble, strive to present it in its real image, i.e. to show its caricatured mask. But I, nevertheless, managed, despite the Chinese caricature, to preserve for myself in all purity the son of Sakkiya, the Buddha". [12, c. 251 - 252]. We recall R. Wagner's reflections on the Grail cup and the human desire to represent everything super-sensual in visual sensual images, including the unearthly source of love. In the commentary to the opera "Lohen-grin" Wagner writes about it, contrasting it with the real reality: "Amidst <...> dreary cares, the eternal thirst for love awoke in human hearts; the more persistent and fiery this thirst became under the burden of reality, the fewer were the opportunities to quench it in this reality" [1, p. 58]. [1, c. 58]. This is how the symbol of the Holy Grail - "existing, but unattainably distant" - appears to them [ibid.], which is the truth comprehended through heavenly love.

Mastering Indian literature helped the composer to cognize himself and comprehend his own spiritual quest. The central concept of Buddhism is nirvana - the ultimate goal of the spiritual path, the highest self-denial. Nirvana means extinction, fading away. The opposite pole to it is samsara, which, in turn, has two interpretations: the cycle of existence, including reincarnations, and the limitedness of the spirit. Nirvana indicates liberation from the infinity of deaths and births, enlightened state, purification from deep suffering. Nirvana is true tranquility, true peace without motion, life's unrest and destructive emotions.

However, the question arises: what does nirvana mean - complete non-existence or transition to a new stage of existence? And here we see a more complicated situation than in Christianity, which undoubtedly speaks of "eternal life", the immortality of the soul, the resurrection and rebirth of redeemed humanity. Nirvana is associated with self-denial, immersion in oneself, renunciation of passions, suppression of the thirst for life, which leads to absolute detachment. The state of nirvana can be achieved both in life and posthumously through merging with the world Brahma; in this case, the individual "I" as if "dissolves" in the universal cosmos. Nirvana is connected with the process of spiritual perfection, and in this again we see a deep kinship between the two religions, since Christian virtue is closely connected with the formation of the inner qualities of man. According to Buddhist wisdom, the state of nirvana cannot be adequately described in words, but can only be experienced. The path outlined in the teachings of the Buddha leads to perfection, but each of the disciples must travel it independently.

The regularity of the interpretation of the opera "Parsifal" through the prism of Buddhist ideas is confirmed by the plot and semantic overlaps with Wagner's sketches of the Buddhist dramatic poem "The Victorious". The French Wagnerologist A. Lishtanberger writes that this sketch clearly outlines the plot of "Parsifal", but in a Hindu version: "Put in place of the Buddhist dogma of nirvana the Christian dogma of renunciation, in place of the community of Buddha - the brotherhood of the Grail Knights, in place of the ascetic Ananda - the "pure-hearted simpleton" Parsifal, in place of the passionately in love Prakriti - Kundri, and you will get almost in all essential features of the drama "Parsifal"" [21, c. 427]. The basis of "The Victorious" is the plot of the legend, which R. Wagner met in the book by E. Bürnuf "Introduction to the History of Indian Buddhism". The plot of the dramatic poem is as follows: Prakriti mockingly rejected the love of the ruler of the Chandal tribe, and for this she was born a Chandal girl in her new life in order to experience the bitterness of unrequited love (equal retribution, a kind of "boomerang of life"). Prakriti is naturally seen as a prototype of Kundry, but the Indian girl pays for the only sin in her past life, not acting as a generalization of Femininity, like the heroine of a Wagnerian drama-mystery. According to the composer's memoirs, in the Indian legend he was interested in the motif of double life, when the past life is felt as an unconditional reality, influencing the present and requiring a decision in the future. Wagner writes: "Before the spiritual gaze of the Buddha, the lives of the beings he meets in all their past births are revealed with the same clarity as their present. A mere legend receives its meaning from the fact that the past lives of the suffering actors are brought, as something immediately contemporary, into the new phase of their being. I immediately realized how to convey the sounding musical motif of double life, and this is what prompted me to dwell with special affection on the idea of creating "The Winners"" [11, p. 273][2] .

Turning to Wagner's diary entries, we can find another important point of contact between the works under consideration, which lies in the interpretation of the nature of Femininity: on October 5, 1858, the composer recounts the cognitive intension that arose when he read Kep-Pen's history of the Buddha's religion. The new source allowed the composer to deepen his own vision of the images he loved, to discover a trait he had not noticed before, which helped him to draw serious conclusions: "Here is this trait: at first Sakkiya-Muni was strongly opposed to the admission of women to the community of saints. Repeatedly he expresses the conviction that women, by nature, are too subordinate to the tasks of the race, too dependent on their moods, too subject to selfishness and the demands of personal life to concentrate and give themselves to those broad contemplations which liberate individuality from its natural tendencies and lead to redemption." [12, c. 252]. Ananda, the Buddha's favorite disciple, managed to persuade the teacher to abandon his harshness and allow women access to the community. A mighty prospect opened up before the composer, in his own words. P. Wagner had previously been worried about how to introduce into the musical and dramatic concept the image of the Buddha, who had

____

2 Indian culture is a late fascination of R. Wagner. Along with the philosophy of A. Schopenhauer, it is found in the composer's "Wahnfried" library, while in the "Dresden" period these sources were not yet part of his reading interests [46, p. 2].

achieved complete freedom and thrown off all his passions. And here a creative insight emerged - this difficulty is overcome, because the spiritual teacher must also go through a new knowledge, giving the heroine the opportunity to achieve the highest sanctity and freedom thanks to her long-suffering love and self-denial.

The above reflections by the composer allow us to draw a parallel between The Victorious and Parsifal due to the mystery background - Kundry's entry into the community of the servants of the holy cup, the heroine's acquisition of the integrity of existence through redeeming the sinfulness of her female nature and ascending to the highest level of understanding of the innermost, forbidden and supersensual. This event, it would seem, contradicts the very nature of the preternatural seductress, the hypnotism of erotic influence, but it is also quite natural, because she herself is seen as a suffering victim caught in the net of voluptuousness. Amfortas and Kundry are united by a spiritual wound that causes them to suffer deeply from their own imperfection, a vice that contradicts their soul's aspiration to the light, each of them longing for healing. Prakriti and Kundri undergo a mysterious journey of discovery and self-discovery of the alternative existence hidden in their nature.

The name of the heroine of the dramatic poem, Prakriti, has in Hinduism the deep ontological meaning of material existence, the opposite of merging with Brahma. The material world, which is referred to in Hinduism by the concept of prakriti, has illusory properties, as a result of which one can fall into the delusion that it is true and there is no other. However, the immortal part of man - purusha - aspires to Brahma, marking the possibility of spiritual formation of the human self on the way to the true foundations of the universe. Taking into account R. Wagner's fascination with Indian literature, it is natural to assume that he was familiar with the meaning of the ancient Indian philosophical concept of prakriti. In any case, the correlation of this succinct Hindu symbol with an Indian name and its semantic coincidence with the characterization of the heroine of the sketch for the drama The Winners, her passionate nature, gives us a deeper insight into the composer's intention. The kinship of the images of Prakriti and Kundry makes it possible to extrapolate the archaic meaning of life's intention to the multifaceted personality of Prazhenshchina in the drama-mystery Parsifal. It is also necessary to separate the two concepts - the wheel of samsara as an endless chain of life cycles and Prakriti as the substance of the natural world, but they are still close to each other, having a point of semantic intersection in their opposition to Nirvana and Brahma, which, in turn, are associated with another pole - self-denial.

In correlation with Prakriti, the image of Kundri is more complex and ambiguous; it is filled with extremely deep symbolism, being a capacious generalization of archetypal meanings. She is a preternatural temptress who feels inner dissatisfaction, longs for purification, soothing and renewal; she waits for her redeemer (the subconscious motive of her behavior), who will give her pure love. As a result, her suffering only intensifies, as no one can resist her charms. In the mystery drama "Parsifal" Klingzor, calling her to himself, does not call her by a single name: "To me! To me! Here! Rise from your sleep; - you, color of temptation! Daughter of the devil! Rose of hell! Herodias was thou,-who else? Gundrigia is there, Cundry is here! Come here! Get up! Kundry! My slave! Appear!" (translated from the German by Vs. Cheshikhin). The plurality of her personality is due to the fact that she is conceptualized by the composer not as a single person, but as a symbol of sinful femininity, striving for Christianity (the knights call her a heathen, a savage), but unable to do so because of her vicious nature, far from spiritual purity and detachment from everything material, carnal and bodily, those manifestations of natural animal life that can humiliate a human being.

At the same time, Wagner does not conceive of bodily-spiritual unity in the light of vice, since true love does not harbor sin. However, the loving hearts in the composer's work strive to overcome life's intention: Wagner's Eros aspires to transcendence. Here we can find an analogy with the philosophy of Plato, who distinguished two Eroses: the Eros of Aphrodite the vulgar and the Eros of Aphrodite the celestial. The first of them is associated with carnal love, satisfaction of lust, the second - with the desire not to be separated from the beloved all his life [31, p. 129 -

130]. Eros in a high understanding is "the manifestation of the immortal beginning in a mortal being" [31, p. 163] [31, с. 163]. The theme of overcoming the sinfulness of the *Venusberg*, which Wagner develops in his commentary on the opera "Tannhäuser", is continued in the plot and musical-dramaturgical solution of the image of Kundry. In the earlier opera, the heroine-temptress appears as a psychologically integral character, the embodiment of "elfish femininity" (according to C. G. Jung) [43, p. 117][3] , her attractiveness initially has natural outlines. The face of Venus is transformed in a kind of crooked mirror, acquiring demonic features in the mirror of Tannhäuser's mental torment: the goddess of sensual love is perceived as a sign of obsession, since she has subjected the knight to her power. However, Venus herself does not need spiritual healing; the contradiction lies in the mismatch between antique morality and Christian morality, in the different ideas of morality and virtue.

It should be noted that despite the archetypal character of Kundry, the composer does not deprive the heroine of purely human feelings and emotions associated with the generalization of life's observations. Her state of mind can be characterized as marginal, extremely tense, on the verge of screaming, then turning into a desperate cry of the soul. Feeling a psychological break, she experiences a fall into the abyss every time. Named Kundry in the opera, she is a slave of voluptuousness, unable to free herself from the chains of the evil magician who manipulates her and turns her

---

3 C. G. Jung associates archaic sensuality with the "elfic life sphere", where Christian moral categories are absent, because in the pagan environment "bodily and mental life are devoid of modesty, do without conventional morality, and from this become only healthier" [43, p. 117]. The connection of Venus with the elfic sphere, identified by the Swiss scholar, coincides with the specificity of its leitmotiv characterization in R. Wagner's opera. It is characterized by a theme in the spirit of *Elfenmusik*, revealing parallels with G. Berlioz's dramatic symphony Romeo and Juliet - Mercutzio's story about the dream fairy Queen Mab. In the French composer's work, the magical realm of the elves, a vivid, scherzo, elusive and elusive image generates programmatic associations with the leap of mythological creatures whizzing through the air. The characterization of Venus and her kingdom is resolved by R. Wagner in the overture's GP in the same figurative and dramaturgical key, and a similar image - the gallop of mythological creatures - involuntarily arises in the perception: swift movement combined with the semantics of the music of elves; percussion, which performs a coloristic and rhythmic function, apparently imitates the ringing of bells. The Wild Ride, the image of the Wild Hunt is the goddess sweeping through the night sky with her retinue. This program-associative series is based on the subjective perception of the musical material by the author of the monograph. However, the scherzo-elvish image of Venus - bright and alluring - does not coincide with the established attributes of the characterization of the role of the heroine-seducer. The enchanting face of the goddess, however, is presented in her arioso, the thematic material of which is recreated in the overture's development episode.

into an instrument of seduction. A savage, in some ways akin to the animal world and at the same time a beautiful seductress, the heroine leads a double life. Signs of split personality - one of the manifestations of the plurality of Prazhenshchina's nature. In the foreground there is unconscious, uncontrolled psychic energy, impulsiveness, impulsiveness, the heroine is equally alien to good and evil; harmony is only potentially conceivable in the depths of this ambiguous being.

In the mystery drama Parsifal, the ideas of compassion and self-denial are embodied in the most generalized form. The ability to empathy (empathy) is born in Parsifal's spiritual life unexpectedly - as a mysterious epiphany. At first he appears immersed in himself, ignorant, free, selfish. Here again we find a point of contact between Christianity and Buddhism, thanks to the archetype of the Path: cognition is always linked to spiritual growth, to processes of maturation and deep self-knowledge. Parsifal has his own path - from ignorance to knowledge, from simplicity to holiness. Jesus says of himself: "I am the way and the truth and the life" [John 14:6]. [Jn. 14: 6]. Similarly, in Indian religious consciousness, the path is equated with knowledge, being, striving for truth. "Isha unipashada" includes reflections on the difficult path of humanity: "O Agni! Lead us along the auspicious path to prosperity, O god who knows all paths. Remove from us the seducing sin. We shall give thee the greatest praise." [37][4] .

In the mystery drama Parsifal, Wagner most consistently pursues the idea of the vanity of sensual existence, Eros, the will to life, contrasting the corporeal and supersensual. The image of Kundry resonates with the philosophical notion of samsara, because in her personality lies the vital energy that prevents the achievement of monastic asceticism in the knightly community of St. Gra-al. Her figure can be interpreted in terms of reincarnation, the idea of reincarnation. Kundri is present in a multitude of personalities and destinies, her samsara is an endless chain of suffering, her plight is the consequences of aggravated karma, she longs for liberation, death, eternal rest and enlightenment. The heroine encompasses multiple

---

4 Agni is fire, one of the most revered Vedic gods, the third of the five bhutas (elements) from which the world is built: akashu (space), air (vayu), fire (agni), water (apas) and earth (bhumi) [7].

selves, she is Woman as such. In this connection, the eradication of the feminine, its transition to the otherworldly level, is seen as a sign of death, because asceticism as the mortification of the will to life leads to personal perfection, nirvana, but renunciation does not contribute to the continuation of the family, the connection of generations, the natural cycle of life (Eros).

It is peace without any movement, unrest and destructive emotions that Kundry and Amfortas long for; each of them suffers in his own way from his own imperfection, which is projected onto the social macrocosm as well - all the Grail knights desire peace and liberation, demonstrating the community's collective aspiration. The Christian image of the repentant sinner has points of contact with mystery teachings: spiritual ascent is always preceded by an inner search, and often by the deepest moral fall, a descent into the abyss. K. K. Svasyan cites an ancient Indian parable, which tells about a young man who wanted to become a disciple of the path.

"Do you know how to lie?" his teacher asked him.

"Of course not," replied the surprised student.

"Do you know how to steal?" the teacher asked again.

"No," exclaimed the young man, blushing with bewilderment.

The third time his teacher asked him, "Do you know how to kill?"

And the third time the answer was given, "No": would I dare to address you if I knew how to do all these things.

The teacher's answer: "Then go and learn to do it, and once you have learned, don't do it" [34, p. 33]. [34, c. 33].

K. C. G. Jung considers the Gnostic hymn about the soul, which is about a son sent by his father-king to retrieve a lost pearl (a symbol of a higher spiritual value, for which the hero goes to his own depths), which is found in the

at the bottom of a deep well guarded by a dragon. The value found there leads the young man, in the end, to the highest bliss [43, p. 109]. To the symbols of this kind, according to the opinion of the Swiss psychologist, should be attributed the castle of the Holy Grail. The way to Montsalvat is connected with the descent - the traveler "is separated from the mountain by an abyss, a narrow and deep precipice, far below the noise of underground waters", and then follows the ascent to the desired shrine [ibid., p. 109-110]. This symbol means the spirit, which aspires to "the highest freedom, soaring above the depths, escape from the prison of chthonic" [ibid., p. 110]. Self-discovery requires courage, only the chosen one is able to find the way out of the terrible depths. The Grail symbolizes, according to C. G. Jung, "man's eternal search for inner integrity, the fullness of existence" [ibid., p. 289] [ibid., p. 289].

As in the dramatic poem "The Victorious", the mystery drama "Parsi- fal" recreates the spiritual path - the ascent to the heights of the spirit is preceded by a descent into the abyss. In both Wagnerian works, the motif of punishment for a past-life offense that must be atoned for is revealed. The mocking laughter, the insult inflicted on Christ, determines the reason for the remissness of the eternal temptress Kundry, who longs to make amends for her sin by constantly recalling the Savior's suffering gaze, filled with love for all mankind.

Prakriti's karma is determined by the torment caused to the rejected lover, for which the heroine herself must experience the torment of unrequited passion. At the same time, payback is commensurate with the offense - the thirst for sensual love, unquenchable, unrequited attraction, which at the same time is a stepping stone to deliverance, so that, having overcome it, she can rise to a new level of understanding of the world. In Kundri's characterization, this motif is transformed and significantly strengthened. Prakriti takes a vow of chastity and enters the Buddhist community, gaining the inner freedom and brotherly love of the ascetic Ananda, who has resisted her charms. Similarly, Kundry achieves inner unity with the Christian principles of the Knights of the Holy Grail through the purity of Parsifal, who did not succumb to the temptations of voluptuousness, but, on the contrary, through mystical insight, developed a sense of compassion for Amfortas that freed the heroine from the shackles of sensuality.

The leitmotif of temptation reveals its hypnotic formula of influence, and temptation itself becomes in Klingzor's hands an instrument of violence against the personality - hence the emphasized somnambulism and unintentional behavior of Kundry. In both Wagnerian narratives, one can find three reference points in the characterization of heroines overcome by passionate attraction: past-life misdeeds → karmic punishment → deliverance from it. The vector direction of the internal development of the female character outlines the spiritual path: in order to find the integrity of existence, one must experience a fall into the abyss (Kundry), a thirst for the resolution of the existing contradiction between the desired, the actual and the necessary (Prakriti).

Parsifal's mission is not only to restore the general harmonic balance that Klingzor has disturbed, to establish order in the community of the Grail Knights, to relieve Amfortas of his physical and mental torment, but also to free the temptress Kundry from the net of sin. The fulfillment of the latter is reflected in the score of Kundry's external and internal actions, recreating the mystery background of the musical drama. It is as if she were waiting for her savior, recognized him, saw something akin to Christ (chaste love), in connection with which her behavior changes radically, pointing to the archetype of the repentant sinner (Mary Magdalene, Lk. 7: 37 - 38), who has finally found peace of mind. The inwardly transformed heroine renounces hopeless emotions, achieving inner balance, purification and renewal. Such a desired peace is outlined in her consciousness through the image of death-redeemer (eternal sleep). Due to the multidimensional archetypal content of the drama-mystery, the denouement is logical from the point of view of meaning formation - nirvana marks the end of the cycle of rebirths so painful for the heroine (Buddhism), while at the same time marking the state of grace (Christianity).

The link between Christianity and Buddhism is the detachment that characterizes the lives of Christian saints and disciples of the Buddha. In Act III of the mystery drama Parsifal, the spiritual transformation of the title character is expressed through silence, marking the severance of psychic ties with the outside world. Kundry also loses the need for verbal communication until her death, which indicates her inner purification, renewal, liberation, and enlightened state, similar in many ways to Eastern meditation, when immersion in one's own depths reaches such a concentration that external impulses no longer affect consciousness. Through their silence Kundry and Parsifal renounce the world and mundane emotions, rising to a new stage of spiritual self-knowledge. Let us recall that silence as a spiritual virtue characterizes the life of hermits in many Christian and Buddhist monastic communities, being an integral part of their way of life. In Act III of Tannhäuser, after praying to her heavenly protector, the Blessed Virgin, Elisabeth becomes silent until the end of her earthly journey, which marks the enlightenment of the redeemer's spirit. In "Parsifal" the plot motif associated with silence as a sign of spiritual transformation acquires a new semantic content, which is due to the genre nature of the mystery, full of mystical content.

Thus, the plot milestones outlined in The Winners receive a semantic multiplication in Parsi-fala (the oriental motifs developed at an earlier stage find, paradoxically, their culminating expression in the Christian drama-mystery that crowns the composer's work) and, at the same time, a double subtext associated with the assimilation of Buddhist and Christian teachings.

Conclusions. The idea of immortality in the work of R. Wagner is contained in the overcoming of life's passions. The vector orientation of the spiritual path leads through knowledge to the sanctification of truth, from the powerlessness of man, when the future is seen in the darkest colors, to the release of the spirit, its creative energy, to overcome the end of life on the way to eternity. In the genre of tragedy and R. Wagner's operas, where the composer took as a basis the model of ancient Greek dramatists, thought of as a standard, the end of life was, paradoxically, a sign of immortality. Catharsis is determined by compassion and the significance of the deeds, actions, feelings and motivations of the protagonist, who, by sacrificing his life, rises above personal emotions and becomes a spokesman for universal values.

In Christianity, the Messiah gives believers hope for immortality through his own path - the agony of the cross on Golgotha, death, and the sacrament of resurrection.

Buddha achieves nirvana through renunciation of the world of illusion. In order to realize holiness and bliss in the realm of transcendental world harmony, one must die to all earthly (material and mortal) things. If in Christianity this majestic idea is illuminated by the inner light of love and compassion, in Buddhism it is colored with a halo of meditative detachment, in ancient Greek tragedy it is a sense of purification, catharsis due to the deepest empathy with the protagonist of the work.

Turning to various sources, the composer saw in them a kind of unity, a reflection of the creative quest of his inner self, which leads to a gradual self-discovery, a gradual disclosure of ideas interpreted variantly , starting with the operas of the 40s right up to Parsifal. The composer's artistic consciousness develops a mechanism of likenesses (which are correspondences, but not identities), which allows him to combine such phenomena as Christianity and Buddhism, the Hellenistic worldview and Schopenhauerian ethics into an inseparable synthesis. Intuitively comprehended by R. Wagner's intuitive understanding of the kinship of religions has its prerequisites in the universalism of religious symbols endowed with universal meaning, helping the composer to express his own unique and distinctive worldview in artistic creation.

The composer's entire operatic oeuvre can be likened to a grandiose metacycle. The idea of immortality acts as the semantic denominator of the composer's creative evolution, subordinating to itself a number of interrelated semantic images: suffering and compassion, sin and redemption, life and death, Eros and Agape, which are juxtaposed in the context of the mythologem of the Path (which can be presented as both a process and a result) - the symbol-equivalent of the spiritual formation of the human self.

However, the very concept of Liebestod, which determines the direction and outcome of the spiritual quest of the Bayreuth master's operatic heroes, reveals an inner contradiction: life is movement, vanity of vanities, a string of sufferings that must be cut short and overcome. Death in Love is not nothingness, because love as the basis of all foundations and the highest truth is part of earthly existence as a process. This is the paradox that prevents the possibility of eternal peace, rest, harmony within the framework of earthly realities, because love is defined by aspiration, process, ascent, becoming. According to R. Wagner's artistic concept, only the union of the lovers' eidos at the metaphysical level in the areola of transcendent world love can be static, enduring, absolutely harmonious. In this connection, Liebestod is conceived by him not as death, but as the immortality of earthly love, which has found its ideal embodiment within the framework of posthumous otherness. Life (movement) and death (statics) are thus not absolute antitheses, but form an inseparable whole united by the idea of immortality.

Thus, the idea of immortality synthesizes various heuristic sources, formed in the cultural and historical experience of mankind. This semantic image receives variant interpretations in R. Wagner's work, starting with the works of the 40s and up to "Parsifal", gradually enriching with new "overtones" - echoes of the composer's cognitive activity.

The Meaning of the Angel as an Archetype in the Works of R. Wagner

Currently, there is a tendency to increase the attention of scholars to the spiritual origins of musical art. Various approaches to this problem are demonstrated by the materials of international scientific conferences published in the collections of articles "Music and the Bible" [29] and "Musical Culture of the Christian World" [27]. [27]. M. Cherkashina's publication considers the Gospel motifs in the opera "Lohengrin" by R. Wagner [39]. G. Kaloshina's works touch upon the scientific problematics related to the refraction of the mysterious beginning and "Christian tragedy" in musical art [17; 18; 19]. N. Gorelik considers the opera "Faust" by Sh. Gounod not only as the first example of lyric opera, but also as a religious and philosophical tragedy [14]. Russian culture is characterized by the appeal to religious and moral values, which is reflected in the musical art. This problematic is revealed in the article by N. Beketova [4]. In the dissertation study by O. Mikhailova, G. Rossini's "Moses" and G. Verdi's "Nebuchadnezzar" are considered from the perspective of identifying the principles of biblical narrative embodiment in the operas of Italian composers of the first half of the 19th century as a conceptual and dramaturgical basis that determines the typological qualities of the works [26].

However, the problem of the realization of the idea of angelic service in the works of the German master has not yet become the subject of scientific research, despite the fact that the meaning of the Angel runs "punctuated" through the entire creative heritage of R. Wagner. The meaning image of the Angel will be considered in accordance with the attitudes of C. G. Jung, who introduced the term archetype into analytical psychology, reflecting, according to his concept, the collective unconscious of mankind. In his scientific research, the Swiss scientist considers biblical and evangelical images as archetypes [44]. Of undoubted interest in the light of the chosen topic of research is also the publication "The Book of Angels", which contains the works of theologians and philosophers [20].

We learn about the essence of angels and their ministry, first of all, from the texts of Holy Scripture. We turn to the etymology of the word "angel", which in Greek means "messenger", "messenger", indicating the kind of mission performed. The Greek word "evangelion" has the root "angel" and means "good news". There is a reciprocal relationship: heavenly angels bring people the message of spiritual salvation. In the Revelation of John the Theologian it is written: "And I saw another angel flying in the middle of heaven, who had the everlasting gospel to preach to them that dwell on the earth, and to every tribe and tribe, and tongue and people" [Rev. 14: 6].

In the miniature "Angel" from R. Wagner's vocal cycle to words by M. Wesen-donk, an unnamed messenger of heaven appears to the tormented Soul at the moment of death, marking its transition from the world of sorrow to the heavenly realm. Wesen-donk, an unnamed messenger of heaven appears to the tormented Soul at the moment of death, marking its transition from the world of sorrow to the heavenly realm. In the New Testament we find evidence of such a ministry. We learn from the words of Christ that at the hour of death the righteous soul is met by angels. In the Gospel according to Luke we read: "The beggar died and was carried by angels to Abraham's bosom" [Luke 16: 22]. Involuntarily we remember M. Lermontov's poem "Angel", which tells about the birth of a man whose soul is carried by an angel to the world of sorrow and tears. The Angel's song will forever remain in the soul of man, in connection with which in earthly life he will be sad about heaven. In the poem by M. Vezendonk, the Angel, on the contrary, takes the Soul from the world of "sorrows and rebellious darkness" (translated by V. Kolomiitsev). In both poetic works, heaven is contrasted with the earthly life of man: the stay in a bodily shell is temporary, as there is eternal life, to which the soul aspires. After death, it returns to its home, where Light and Love reign.

In the work of A. Pushkin we find a through theme connected with the heroes-symbols - a demon and an angel. In 1823, the Russian poet wrote a poem "Demon", where he conveyed skepticism, life disappointments, presenting them in a symbolic form - the mythological character demon, ko varnoy tempter, who visited him since his youth. The description of the demon, which personifies the soul of the disappointed hero, makes us remember the characterization of Eugene Onegin from

Pushkin's novel in verse of the same name. The poet began work on the "encyclopedia of Russian life" in 1823 and completed it in 1831. In 1827 A. Pushkin wrote the poem "Angel" (dedicated to E. Vorontsova), which is a response to the previously written poem "Demon". The mythological character angel represents the image of the beloved, who makes the hero, burdened by the demon, believe in the existence of light, love, helping him to soar with his soul to heaven. We also recall A. Pushkin's lines from Tatiana's letter ("Eugene Onegin"): "Who are you, my guardian angel, / Or an insidious tempter: / Resolve my doubts". In the light of the Russian poet's cross-cutting issues, the juxtaposition of mythological characters in this poetic fragment, which is in unity with the characteristics of Onegin and Tatiana, is perceived in the given context in the light of the theme that always worried the poet. Thus, in Wagner and Pushkin, the mythological character Angel is the personification of femininity, which delivers the suffering soul (male) from demonic obsession / delusion. In this connection we involuntarily recall the paired characters of Wagner's operas of the 40s - the hero-sinner and his redeemer - Glo-lander and Senta, Tannhäuser and Elisabeth. In Wagner, such a correlation between male and female within the mystery of redemption is found in a stripped-down form until Parsifal.

In R. Wagner's vocal cycle with lyrics by M. Wesendonck. The song with the symbolic title "Der Engel" (The Angel) acts as an initio. It opens the opus, which unites a number of songs, each of which is filled with philosophical meaning. This fact may serve as one of the proofs of the significance of the meaningful image of the Angel in the work of the German master. In the vocal miniature the composer outlines the mystery "graphics" - the opposition between the worlds of the lower and upper worlds and their conjunction.

The heroes of R. Wagner's operas have features that allow us to classify them into a single group associated with the interpretation of the meaning of the Angel as a transversal archetype in the work of the German composer. Thus, Senta, Elisabeth and Parsi- fal appear as spiritual mediators between sinners and the Almighty thanks to the power of empathy. The heavenly messenger Lohengrin appears in the opera as

Elsa's guardian angel and her intercessor. The Grail Knights in the operas Lo-engrin and Parsifal can be correlated with the heavenly host, which in Holy Scripture are angels. In addition, in these works the Grail Knights are shown as servants of the holy relic - the cup in which the Savior's blood was collected.

The mediator between the will of the gods and the fate of man is the Valkyries, messengers of death, who, according to ancient Scandinavian mythology, take the souls of dead warriors to Valhalla. Whoever has seen their fiery gaze is destined to die soon ("The Valkyrie" by R. Wagner, Scene IV of Act II - dialog between Siegmund and Brünnhilde). In Wagner's work, the "dialog" of pagan and Christian motifs is repeatedly realized, which makes it possible to correlate the winged harbingers of Scandinavian mythology with the Angels in Christianity. In addition, representations of Angels exist not only in Judaism and Christianity: "They constituted the entourage of the Greco-Roman gods. The image of angels as winged creatures goes back to their eastern prototypes; their prototype is often considered to be Nika" [35, p. 32]. Unlike Christianity, polytheistic religions were interested in the integration of religions. For example, U. Kinzle writes about the existing practice of Roman conquerors identifying their own gods with the ancient Germanic adequates [47, p. 66]. In this regard, the Valkyries can be put in the same row with the listed prototypes of Christian Angels. Their relative similarity with the Christian messengers, servants of the Lord - mediation between the gods and man, the function of messengers, traveling on a winged horse through the air - in this case does not mean identity.

Angels can be on the side of good as well as evil. Demons or devils are angels who in their pride have rebelled against God. They seek to harm His favorite creation - man. This is explained by the fact that in Christianity, angels and people are endowed with freedom of choice, in connection with which the fallen angels are on the side of evil. The images of Loge and Ortruda belong to the luciferic type, as they tempt their victims with the power of evil reasoning (pride of intellect), opposite to the true principles of the universe - Love, intuitive following the Truth. The conflict in the

Dutchman's soul has a luciferic character, as he makes a daring challenge by actualizing the curse associated with pride, in this case human pride. In the Christian scale of moral values, his transgression is sinful. The image of Klingzor reveals a godly motif. He challenges the realm of the Grail, associating himself with the fallen angel Lucifer. His figure is sinister and tragic at the same time. The villain's road to the coveted abode of goodness and light is forever closed to him, which evokes dark vengeful feelings in his soul, since this is what all his actions and aspirations were directed towards. The Dutchman's sinfulness can be redeemed by a faithful loving woman, while the sorcerer has no excuse and no way back, which creates a desperate anger in him.

Let us dwell in more detail on the musical and stage characterization of Elisabeth ("Tannhäuser"). In her image the composer harmoniously combines angelic and human traits. The image of the angelic maiden Elisabeth corresponds in the opera with the image of the Holy Virgin Mary - her heavenly intercessor, about whom Gregory Palamas wrote: "Wishing to create an image of perfect beauty and to clearly show angels and men the power of His art, God truly made Mary the most beautiful. He combined in Her the individual traits of beauty which He gave to other creatures, and made of Her the common adornment of beings visible and invisible, or rather, He made of Her as if a mixture of all the perfections, divine, angelic and human, the highest beauty adorning both worlds, ascending from earth to heaven and even surpassing the latter." [quoted in: 5, p. 3][5] . By nature, Wagner's Elisabeth is truly human. This is evidenced by the aria-characterization of the heroine, full of vitality, which does not allow us to interpret her as a person devoid of earthly aspirations. Tannhäuser's inner conflict, connected with the impossibility of independent liberation from the enchanting attraction to the grotto of Venus, determines the impossibility of the dream of a marriage union - the maiden-angel (this is how the title character of the opera calls her at the moment of bitter remorse) sublimates her own femininity, the potential possibility of motherhood and even her very life in the

---

5 Thus, Gregory Palamas juxtaposes 2 worlds - visible and invisible, material and spiritual, human and angelic.

act of redemptive sacrifice. And in doing so, she reveals her transcendental essence. The spiritual mission of Wagner's heroine corresponds with the archetype (according to C. G. Jung) of her heavenly patroness.

"Blessed among wives," the Virgin Mary is the intercessor of repentant sinners. Let us remember her humanity: according to one of the Apocrypha, the Virgin Mary descends to sinners in hell. As a divine *mediator* (Latin *mediatrix*), she leads the penitent to God, who grants them eternal bliss. Elizabeth's chastity goes back to the Christian symbol of "the eternal virgin who conceived immaculately" [44, p. 198] [44, c. 198]. The heroine is depicted in the opera in the light of exultant youth - Elizabeth's Exit. In addition, according to R. Wagner's author's remark, Tannhäuser's first song, praising the charms of bodily love, evokes contradictory emotions in her (in contrast to her Wartburg surroundings), as "Elizabeth's face reflects a struggle of feelings - admiration mixed with timid surprise" (translation by Viktor Kolomiitsev, Parisian edition of the opera).

Senta is also the Angel Maiden. The composer calls her Angel through the mouth of the Dutchman, and in the final scene of the opera the heroine herself also calls herself the Angel of her beloved - the cursed wanderer - realizing her redemptive mission. The angelized lovers can be compared to the Angel from the eponymous song of R. Wagner's vocal cycle on poems by M. Wesendonck. The spiritual destiny of each of these opera heroines is connected with the transition of the hero-sinner from the world of sorrows to the kingdom of heaven, which turns out to be possible thanks to the boundless Love of the Woman.

In the Faust Overture (1840), R. Wagner embodied the idea of angelic service at the musical and intonational level through the imagery and dramaturgical spheres corresponding to the "Faustian", "Mephistophelean" and "eternally feminine" principles. In this work, the composer presented the themes that run through his work - the struggle between good and evil in the hero's soul, spiritual fall and redemption. It should be recalled that in Goethe's tragedy of the same name the main character in the final scene is carried to heaven by singing angels and in the guise of an angel he is met in paradise by his beloved Margaret, who has atoned for her sins and Faust through Love.

God's work of redemption is concerned with the deliverance of mankind from the shackles of sinfulness. The spiritual mystery takes on enormous proportions in Christianity because of the key significance of the repentant sinner, whose return to the heavenly home is a significant event for the Lord and his angels. In the Gospel according to Luke, Jesus says: "It is not the healthy who have need of a physician, but the sick. I have not come to call the righteous, but sinners to repentance." [Luke 5: 3132]. The parable of the Prodigal Son and the biblical account of Job's trials are also illustrative.

Wagner's operas reveal a mystery graphic, according to which following the immersion into the dark depths of the inner human self is possible:

- ascending to the highest stage of spiritual formation (The Flying Dutchman, Tannhäuser);

- the final fall, the loss of inner unity with the source of true being (Wotan, partly Elsa).

The Holy Scriptures refer to the holy ministers of God as "angels of light". The idea of luminosity is manifested by the names of angels. Thus, Lucifer in Latin means light-bearer [35, p. 325], the name of Archangel Uriel has Hebrew roots and translates as "God is my light" [20, p. 75]. [20, c. 75]. According to theology, the fallen angels lose their connection with the world source of light, their fate is eternal darkness. The Lord in the Christian worldview is the source of heavenly Light. St. Gregory Palamas, Metropolitan of Solunsk (XIV century.) wrote about the luminosity of the Angels, involved in the original divine light: "Angel is the first light nature after the first cause, from which receives the brilliance and the second light, flowing from the first light and participating in it. And circularly moving divine minds unite in the beginningless and infinite brilliance of goodness and beauty." [20, c. 546]. In R. Wagner's work, the archetype of light as a semantic sign of transcendental world harmony is defined by the composer's comprehension of the unity of love and death from the perspective of Christian mystery. The breakthrough into the unknowable world, the ascent to the Light of Heaven[6] is revealed through the semantic image of Liebestod. Even in the drama "Tristan and Isolde", where the composer appeals "to the image of the mythical Night" [38, p. 369]. [38, p. 369] as the primordial source of life, the semantic image of the posthumous overcoming of the burden of earthly passions is revealed by the semantics of transcendental radiance, which acts as a stable iconic unit in the composer's work, beginning with The Flying Dutchman and ending with the drama-mystery Parsifal. The exception is The Meistersingers of Nuremberg, where, nevertheless, the ultimate triumph of justice generates a cathartic *enlightened* [italics mine - O. S.] feeling in the recipient's soul.

The intonational emblem of light is presented on a semantic level in the introduction to the opera Lohengrin[7] . The semantics of the preternatural celestial radiance is revealed by the harmony of the sustained *A-dur* 'treson in the shimmering timbre of the strings and woodwinds in a wide arrangement in a very high register. The transcendence of sound is achieved by the flageolets of the 4 solo violins, dynamic forks within a muted sound (*pp, p*), and subtle timbre transitions, which together create a sense of inner vibration and are associated with gently flowing heavenly grace. A special semantic load is carried by the absence of lower register instruments in the sound score of the fragment, which causes exceptional transparency, floating weightlessness, actualizing the idea of the mysterious graphics of the high world opposed to the low world.

The idea of effulgence is personified in Wagner's operas. In Lohengrin it is manifested in the stage images of the heavenly messenger and his angelized beloved. In Act II Scene II, Elsa's effulgence is actualized in the musical and stage space: her

6 Heaven in the Bible has not only a cosmic, but also a symbolic interpretation. A. Glagolev writes about the symbolic meaning of the Hebrew word *schamaim*: "In this sense it contains the concept of the spiritual world and its mysterious life, in contrast to the earth, which is the environment of sensual life" [20, p. 55].
7 S. Tyshko detects a similar intonation and semantic phenomenon in Mussorgsky's operas, characterizing it as the style of the Favor light [36]. M. Mussorgsky, to all appearances, inherited R. Wagner, who addressed similar intonational means in the introduction to "Lohengrin": "P. Tchaikovsky and A. Serov were delighted with "Lohengrin" and especially with the new orchestral effect, strikingly similar to what we observed in Mussorgsky: strings and winds in the highest register, pp" [36, pp. 430-44]. [36, C. 430-431]. "Lexema of light" is singled out in the musical theater of N. A. Rimsky-Korsakov by A. Zhdanko outside the address to the Christian mystery semantics [16].

white garment, light-bearing cantilena, spatial localization - she stands on the balcony as if she were soaring above the sinful earth. Her heavenly countenance is emphasized by the opposition of Friedrich and Ortrude, who, according to the composer's remark, are dressed in dark clothes; their statements rely on semantic signs of evil fantasy, the genre prototype of the revenge aria; they look upwards and downwards at Elsa. R. Wagner's detailed authorial instructions regarding this scene and the musical semantics are intended to convey the social metamorphosis of Friedrich and Ortrud, which is connected with their banishment from Brabant, on the one hand, and their belonging to the world of evil fantasy, on the other. Elsa's arioso reveals the heroine's unearthly countenance; she confides the secret of her heart to the wind; the girl is characterized by the composer as naive and pure (not of this world); she is absolutely the same here as in the court scene. One could argue that life has taught her nothing. First and foremost, not to trust those who have already done evil. The heroine's descent to the demonic character, like Lohengrin's descent to earth has a symbolic. A parallel can be drawn indirectly with the tradition of Baroque rhetorical musical figures associated with the semantics of descending into the abyss (*catabasis, passus duriusculus*).

In the author's programmatic explanations to the overture to The Flying Dutchman, Wagner characterizes Senta's gaze as a *light* [italics mine - *O. Sh.*] beckoning the suffering hero-sinner, filled with "*divine* [italics mine - *O. Sh.*] sympathy and longing" [1, p. 56]. [1, c. 56]. Given that in the opera the heroine is verbally characterized as an angel, it can be argued that in the author's programmatic explanations the composer is addressing the semantic image of the Divine Light, to which the messengers of heaven belong.

Parsifal's luminosity is associated with biblical and Christian ideas about the Messiah, the redeemer of mankind's sins, with the sacred symbol of the Holy Grail cup, faith and mental purity. His image summarizes R. Wagner's artistic experience, combining the features of the angelized redeemers Senta, Elisabeth and the heavenly messenger Lohengrin.

Radiance is inherent in the image of Siegfried. It would seem that this hero is far from the Christian tradition, in contrast to Lohengrin and Parsifal. However, there is still a link between the ideas of Christianity and the image of Siegfried. P. Wagner characterizes Siegfried as a fearless radiant hero. Jesus says of himself: "I am the light of the world; whoever follows me will not walk in darkness, but will have the light of life" [John 8: 12]. [John 8: 12]. The archetype of solar / light-bearing is associated in the world culture with the ideas of goodness and purity. The Sun is the source of life, which has long been worshiped.

The lightness of the fearless hero is revealed in the tetralogy through the phonics of the major triad, which symbolizes the purity of the laws of the natural world. In this connection it is appropriate to relate the introductions to "Lohengrin" and "The Gold of the Rhine", since they reveal the beginning of beginnings - the logos-Light and the substance-Water. The composer presents the profound idea of the primordial basis of the world in a variety of ways, going back to Christian and pre-Christian ideas. In both cases it is revealed by the phonics of the major triad. The beginning of beginnings symbolizes in R. Wagner the idea of truth, allowing the composer to postulate it on an intonational level through the sacred sign of the chorale and the heroic fanfare. Wagner links the sunny Siegfried, reunited with Brünnhilde, with the redemptive foundations of the universe [12, p. 180]

The vocal miniature "Sorrow" from R. Wagner's vocal cycle to poems by M. Wesendonck merges two meanings of the symbol of the sun - the cosmic luminary (with a "plus" sign) and the day, ruthless society (with a "minus" sign) - that are characteristic of the German composer's work. The song opens with an exclamation of despair at the word *sun* (*Sonne*). It is possible that the beginning of the song is the impulse that inspired the image-symbol of society in the drama Tristan und Isolde. Two contrasting beginnings are noticeable in the song: Tristanian sorrows, highlighted by the initial dissonant consonance and the rhetorical figure of *catabasis*, and the metaphor of the sun as a "hero in the rays of victories" - a heroic fanfare akin to the leitmata of the light-bearing Siegfried.

The affinity of Siegfried the hero with the Christian Messiah is revealed in the verbal text of Act III of the penultimate day of the tetralogy - in the rapturous duet of the heroes singing praises to Sieglinde, who gave Siegfried life, to the native land that nourished him, to the gaze of the Valkyrie, thanks to which he recognized bliss and to the light-bearing hero-redeemer himself:

Siegfried

(in a burst of the greatest delight):

Oh, glory be to mother,

Who gave me life,

And the earth,

Who nurtured me!

I saw your eyes

And in him I recognized bliss!

Brunhilde

(with great excitement)

Oh, kudos to her,

who gave birth to you,

Oh, kudos to her,

who nourished you!

Only you could come to me,

You were the only one who could interrupt my dream!

Light [italics mine - *O.S.*] Siegfried! Siegfried!

You bring life

By the light [italics mine - *O.S.*] of your own!

(translated from German by V. Kolomiytsev)

Analogies also arise with the Gospel sayings about the Virgin Mary. Elizabeth, filled with the Holy Spirit, exclaimed: "blessed art thou among wives, and blessed is the fruit of thy womb!" [Lk. 1: 42]; the woman who was listening to the preaching of Jesus said in illumination: "blessed is the womb that bore You, and the teats that nourished You!" [Lk. 11: 27].

The idea of redemption is linked in Wagner with the idea of the unity of sensual love and self-denial. Only in "Parsifal" is erotic love, which the author thinks of as a troublemaker, completely supplanted by fraternal sobornost. In the opera Lohengrin, the heavenly messenger longs to find the love of an earthly woman. His loneliness acts as a kind of assonance to the mental torment of Jesus, who finds no empathy even among his closest disciples - the Apostles. Let us remember the Savior's bitterness when his disciples fell asleep at the hour when his soul was overwhelmed with grief and foreboding of death, and he cried out to the Lord that this cup might pass him by!

Let us also refer to a biographical fact cited in the monograph by A. Lishtanberger, who points to the mystical experience of the composer's contact with the angelic world at the moment of writing the Parsi- fal mystery drama. Lishtanberger, who points to the mystical experience of the composer's contact with the angelic world at the time of writing the drama-mystery Parsi- fal. In the spring of 1857, on Good Friday contemplating the festive nature, Wagner was suddenly illuminated by an intuition of the mystery of Christ; it seemed to him (as he told H. P. von Wolzogen[8]) that he heard angels singing: "putting aside for a while the score of Tristan, he wrote those verses full of some mystical tenderness, in which Gurnemanz tells Parsifal about the charms of Holy Friday" [21, c. 427]. The core idea of "Parsifal" was found.

The composer directly turned to the Gospel when sketching for the drama Jesus of Nazareth (1848), where he expressed his own vision of the radiant face of the Savior, quite different from the prevailing canonical views. His unprecedented attention to this source is evidenced by numerous notes, which is considered by M. Eger as a rare

---

8 Hans Paul von Wolzogen was the author of the term "leitmotif" and a passionate admirer of R. Wagner's work.

exception, since the master was very careful with his books [46, p. 3]. The composer's creativity is permeated with biblical and evangelical motifs, relying on the essential foundations of Christian faith. However, the attitude of Wagner the artist to religion was complex and very ambiguous, reflected in the statements concerning the theme of the creator's path from religion to art, recorded in Cosima's diaries. Thus, according to the composer's conviction, art can refer to religious symbols, but it should do so "freely, freeing them from dogmatic seriousness" [cited in: 45, 45, 45, 45, 45]. [cited in: 45, p. 22].

R. Wagner interpreted religious symbols through the prism of the idea of Kunstreligion. Wagner interpreted religious symbols through the prism of the idea of Kunstreligion. *The* use of symbols in the German composer's operatic works does not lead to the loss of their deep meaningful content. According to the Bayreuth master's conviction, art revives them, giving them new life. Art thus assumes the high mission of religion.

Thus, the archetype of the Angel appears in R. Wagner's work in various semantic readings, revealing itself in the idea of luminosity, mystery graphics of the "high" and "low" worlds, determining the direction of the inner formation of the opera heroes who act as spiritual mediators on the way to finding redemption for the suffering soul.

The Mystery of Redemption as a Path of Knowledge and Self-Knowledge in R. Wagner's Ring of the Nibelung Tetralogy

R. Wagner's Ring of the Nibelung tetralogy has not previously been analyzed from the standpoint of its embodiment of the mystery of redemption. Meanwhile, the legitimacy of such an interpretation of the grandiose opera cycle is confirmed by the composer's reflection.

The mystery drama Parsifal is the logical conclusion of the Bayreuth genius' work, which is deeply Christian in its foundations. In his operas of the 1940s the composer turns to Christian legends. In his interpretations of Christian legends we invariably encounter pagan motifs. When choosing primary sources for his operas, R. Wagner often prefers to turn to the Apocrypha. In Parsifal, for example, he interprets the symbol of the Holy Grail cup, which is absent from the canonical Gospel texts; it belongs to an apocryphal version of the Gospel - the Gospel according to Nicodemus.

The meaning image of redemption is not narrowly localized in Wagner's work. Wagner's reflection reveals reflections that clearly testify to his inclusion of Christian ideas in the semantic "aura" of the tetralogy, despite the fact that the primary source of the grand opera cycle was Scandinavian mythology. In scientific thought, the opinion that the semantic content of this work is much broader than the archaic source: in Wagner's tetralogy, scientists saw the embodiment of "the philosophy of history in sounds" [28, p. 9], as well as "the philosophy of history in sounds" [28, p. 9]. [28, p. 9], reinterpretation of ancient Greek mythological motifs, in particular, the trilogy "Prometheus" by Aeschylus [48]. T. Mann wrote that in the tetralogy the composer combined the incommunicable: psychology and myth: "Their compatibility is tried to be denied, psychology is considered something too rational not to see it as an insurmountable obstacle on the way to the land of the mythical. It is accepted to oppose the mythical, as it is accepted to oppose it to music, although this very com plex - the combination of psychology, myth and music - in two striking cases, in Nietzsche and in Wagner, appears to us as a living reality" [25, p. 108]. [25, c. 108]. A. Lishtanberger writes about the polarity of worldview attitudes in the considered work - "between enthusiasm and despondency, between love and disgust for life, between Feuerbach and Schopenhauer" [21, pp. 297 - 297]. [21, pp. 297 - 298], R. Wagner "embodied first more of Siegfried's side, then more of Wotan's" [21, pp. 298] [21, c. 298].

In a letter to August Reckel, Wagner calls Siegfried, reunited with Brünnhilde, the redeemer of mankind, and calls the heroine "the conscious redeemer of the world" [12, p. 180]. [12, c. 180]. The definition of the role of Siegfried and Brünnhilde as redeemers of mankind and the world allows us to complete the semantic chain in the context of the mystery of redemption: Loge - temptation, Wotan - the ascent to the truth, ending in collapse. According to A. Losev, in Wagner's tetralogy myth is in interaction with Christian foundations, as in the final scene the composer addresses the Christian idea of redemption [22, p. 26].

It should be noted, however, that the meanings contained in Wagner's tetralogy are much broader than Christian dogma, since they appeal to the universal spiritual and cognitive experience of humanity, depicted, in particular, in pagan myths. Thus, Loge is a representative of Chaos, which in the mythological picture of the world is always fraught with Cosmos, as the element of world discord and destruction is always ready to turn to its creative side.

In myths, the problem of moral choice and moral responsibility is often not as acute as in Christianity, because paganism has different criteria of behavior. In ancient tales, strength and dexterity win, and in this connection we can recall the powerful Wotan and Loge, who is cunning in the realization of deceitful plans.

The formation of Christian morality is rooted in the Old Testament teaching, which, despite the existing continuity, is not identical to the humanism of the New Testament. Thus, according to the Bible, the regulating beginning of human moral behavior is fear before the right hand of the Lord, because the Creator appears not only as a merciful Almighty, but also as a merciless Judge, punishing all those who maliciously violate his covenants: remember the Flood, the destruction of Sodom and Gomorrah. In the Gospel, the loving Father does not punish sinners, but gives mankind the opportunity for repentance and posthumous redemption. Love, not fear, must now guide the choice of the righteous path. In the tetralogy Wotan appears as a truly pagan god who is at the mercy of selfish aspirations. The opposite pole is world love, which alone can redeem the world from sinfulness and save it from final destruction. In the Gospel according to John the way of salvation is shown by means of a symbol, which is the life-giving spring. Thus, when Jesus addressed the Samaritan woman who came to draw water from the well, he revealed to her the meaning of divine love. He contrasts earthly thirst with living water, which symbolizes imperishable spiritual truth that can quench eternal thirst [John 4: 13-14]. Love in the tetralogy also appears as an original and timeless value, opposite to everything finite.

Wagner's artistic worldview combines two categories associated with Christian ideas of God, who is Love and Eternity. The meaning of Liebestod turns out to be consonant with Christianity, as it is associated with posthumous peace and bliss. In the tetralogy, love, cosmic in its scale, encompasses all manifestations of life, starting from its simplest forms (natural philosophical interpretation) and ending with the highest stage - human consciousness.

In Christianity, God is the creator of all things, defining the meaning of all his creatures - small and great, the created world and the world of entities, as represented by the heavenly angels. The aspiration for comprehensiveness and scale in recreating the world cosmos characterizes the world picture of the tetralogy, starting from the logos-substance and ending with the highest ontological manifestations. In the tetralogy, R. Wagner raises and solves questions that are answered by myth, philosophy and religion. In particular, the problems of the structure of the universe, moral choice, ways of cognition and self-knowledge.

Christian faith and mystical intuition, as the guiding forces of inner self-knowledge, are capable of overcoming all kinds of obstacles that are natural in the corruptible world. True believers, according to the Gospel according to Mark, will be accompanied by these signs: in the name of Christ they will cast out demons, speak with new tongues; take up serpents; and if they drink anything deadly, it will not hurt them; lay hands on the sick, and they will be well [Mk. 16: 17-18]. The example of faith commanded by Jesus is refracted in R. Wagner's work in the images of the angelized intercessors Senta and Elizabeth, who atone for the sins of the beloved through spiritual purity and the power of compassion. The light of the maiden-angel's heavenly love frees the Dutchman from a heavy curse. The motif of Christian faith overcoming those obstacles that seem impossible to overcome in the material world is embodied especially vividly in the opera Tannhäuser: the protagonist is saved by the immense love of a woman, the proof of which is a *miracle - a* staff that has turned green. The fundamentally impossible turns out to be achievable. At the same time, this ending of the opera (recall that in the legend Tannhäuser in despair returns to a sinful life, to the goddess of sensual love) has a deep symbolism of resurrection and renewal (the dead branch has awakened to new life). In R. Wagner, the life of the spirit is closely connected with the natural existence of the universe, which is confirmed by the pantheism of the tetralogy, on the one hand, and the Christian drama-mystery Parsifal (the miracle of Good Friday), on the other.

The image of the saintly simpleton in the opera Parsifal, who achieves sacredness through mercy, is close to the images of angelized lovers in the operas of the 1940s. His empathy is stronger than the temptations of the mortal world, overcoming the shackles of sensuality. The path of redemption is revealed in Wagner's work not only in individual and personal mystery, but also on a universal scale: the purification of the sinful world by the power of cosmogonic love in "The Ring of the Nibelung", realized by Brünnhilde; the restoration of world harmony through the compassion of an innocent soul in "Parsifal"; the redemption of the sinfulness of the Venusian mountain in "Tannhäuser". An unattainable goal for the mighty head of the pagan pantheon turned out to be realized by his daughter through her aspiration for world love[9].

____

9 Let us recall that in Christianity God is Light, Truth, and Love, which seems to be the connecting thread between Christian ideas and the work of R. Wagner. In his operas, love, comprehended on an individual-personal level, invariably acts as a creative world-redeeming intension due to the synergy of moral self-

The life journey of Brünnhilde and the luminous Siegfried is inextricably linked to the life-giving forces of nature, which appear as the true measure of truth. "In the beginning was the Word" - so says the canonical translation of the prologue of the Gospel of John, realized by M. Luther in the XVI century. In the Greek text there is the word "logos", which has multiple meanings. I. G. Herder in his commentary to the Gospel (1775) noted that it can be translated in different ways: thought, word, will, action, love [2, p. 650]. In the tetralogy the original, the primary basis of the world is revealed from a naturphilosophical perspective - as a symbol of life-giving nature, cosmogonic Eros. This semantic image is embodied musically: the initial passage through the sounds of the overtone series, then passing into figurations that ascend in their progressive movement to new, ever more powerful energy levels. The *Vorspiel* to "Gold of the Rhine" is a primordial image of being, containing all the impulses of the formation of natural life. Cosmogony, conceptualized as the process of the birth of all things from the water substance, finds, as shown in the tetralogy, embodiment in various forms of being, outlining their diversity, as natural life reveals itself in movement, development, ascent, reaching its peak in human consciousness, thinking, volition, deeds, love. The idea of gradual germination is found in the structure of the leitmotif system: it is an endless accumulation of ever new meanings through the thematic derivation of leitmotifs and their symphonic development. This process reflects the expansion and deepening of knowledge in the context of comprehending the main idea of the work

- from empiricism in the introduction to The Gold of the Rhine to philosophical generalization in Brünnhilde's final monologue.

The Christian mystery is connected with the overcoming of egoism, the choice of love as the initiating moral principle, and the aspiration of the spirit to the true foundations of existence. This path is prefigured in the texts of the New Testament, the commandments of Jesus, who reveals to Christians his own mission as a guide between the human sinful present and its overcoming: "I am the way, and the truth,

---

knowledge, which implies the unity of two energies - man and the universe (in the tetralogy) / man and God (in the interpretation of Christian legends).

and the life." [John 14: 6]. At the same time, there is no identity here, since the foundations of the Christian worldview come into contact in the tetralogy with pagan pantheism and natural philosophical views. It should be noted that in R. Wagner the life of nature and spirit are inseparably linked. For example, the idea of redemption in "Tannhäuser" and "Parsifal" is connected with the spring awakening of nature - the staff that has turned green ("Tannhäuser"), the miracle of Good Friday, when nature itself let Gurnemanz know about the redemption of mankind ("Parsifal").

In the text of the New Testament, let me remind you, the life-giving spring is shown as a succinct symbol that embodies Christian spirituality [John 4: 13-14]. In the tetralogy, the source of truth and life is shown in a different way: the empirical image of the Rhenish water jets acts as a symbol of nature - the natural measure and regulator of moral behavior.

In the tetralogy, moral self-discovery is realized by Wotan and Brünn-Gilde. The descendants of Welze strive for the Eros of natural existence. Wotan embarks on a different path connected with the violation of the laws of love/nature. The reflection of the Father of the World is the antithesis of the immediacy of his descendants' feelings.

The image of Siegfried in Wagner's interpretation, despite its contradiction to Christian ideas (it contains a boldness of spirit inherent in Christian ideals), still contains iconic features, like a halo surrounding his shining face. E. Sadovnikova writes about the problem of iconicity and its refraction in N. A. Rimsky-Korsakov's opera The Tale of the Invisible City of Kitizh and the Virgin Fevronia. She notes that this quality characterizes the hagiography of the righteous, martyrs, works of painting and verbal descriptions. Iconic features are also found in the characteristics of opera characters and the dramaturgy of the musical and stage work she is considering. Iconicity is not related only to the phenomenon of the Orthodox cult, as it is also found in biblical verbal texts belonging to the Judaic tradition, where there was no tradition of pictorial reproduction of religious symbolism [33].

From the point of view of iconicity, hagiography and righteousness, one can draw a parallel between the forest maiden Fevronia and the child of the forest expanses Parsi-fal. It is possible to continue this chain - the forest maiden Snegurochka, unsophisticated in worldly matters, and the forest boy Siegfried. Despite the variant differences, these characters represent a single archetype in many ways; they are the pure children of Mother Nature, uncontaminated in their thoughts and motives thanks to their isolation from the negative influences of society. Iconic features are evident in the angelic countenances of Senta and Elisabeth and define the sacral image of the heavenly messenger Lohengrin and the saintly simpleton Parsifal, as the characters named seem to be surrounded by a glowing halo of sinlessness. The musical and stage portraits of Wagner's heroes, their musical and verbal characteristics, the leitmotif system, meaning formation, and stage action are clearly marked by the signs of Eternity and timelessness inherent in both Christian symbolism and pre-Christian myth, which makes it possible to discover one of the points of contact between them.

Like Christ, Siegfried is a savior, a Messiah, whose birth was foretold in advance, whose atoning death, foretold by the prophetic runes, whose purity and innocence of thought allow us to place him on a par with the holy martyrs, he is a kind of "lamb of God" who was slain on the sacrificial fire. Let us recall the traitorous murder, followed by the realization of what has happened and the symbolically meaningful scene of burial in the purifying flames. However, the life of Christ and the luminous Siegfried should not be entirely identified. In Christianity, God the Father sacrificed the Son out of love for humanity. Siegfried, on the contrary, perishes as a result of the viciousness of Wotan's views and of the world created by this progenitor (microcosm and macrocosm are correlated here according to the principle of image and likeness), because the Father of the world sacrifices the lives of his children for his own salvation.

The tetralogy combines two facets of human cognition and worldview - logic and intuition. Wotan subordinates the fate of the world to the arguments of reason, not trusting the impulses of the heart; he is a reflective hero. Erda's wisdom is determined by the subordination of her thinking to unconscious somnambulism, because her prophecies are the result of the subconscious working in the form of mystical visions. In this connection her utterances have an otherworldly and hypnotic character. Her thinking reproduces the eternal knowledge arising in the form of dreams, where the truth is not the result of cause-and-effect relationships of links in the chain of reasoning (as in Wotan), but the result of subconsciousness. Hence the mysteriousness of her speeches. That which is hidden in Erda's eternal reveries cannot be comprehended through logic, it must be experienced, it must open up one's inner spiritual self to it, as Brünnhilde did when she gave in to an immediate inner impulse to stand up in defense of the Welsungs. Brünnhilde's path of knowledge is in harmony with Erda's eternal reveries - the laws that govern the world and cannot be violated with impunity. Along with showing the real world in all its sensual multicolors, Wagner sought to express in the tetralogy the unconscious - the world of dreams. The extra-rational cognition, which proves inaccessible to the heuristic quest of the Father of the World, is achieved by Brünnhilde. According to gender psychology, the feminine (femininity) is determined by intuitiveness, while the masculine (muscularity), on the contrary, is determined by the structured consciousness. A similar idea was expressed by C. Levi-Strauss, who connected femininity and muscularity with the development of culture - he represented "culture as a superimposition of a discrete dimension on a continuous reality" [cited in: 32, 32, 32, 32]. [cited in: 32, p. 293], and everything continuous, intuitive, irrational is usually identified with the feminine and, on the contrary, everything discrete, rational - with the masculine [ibid.].

In the tetralogy, Wotan, Siegfried, and Brünnhilde travel the path of knowledge and self-discovery. Each of them has his own path to the truth, which determines the final point of their life journey. The deepest tragedy of Wotan and the tetralogy as a whole lies in the impossibility of saving the old world. It can only be redeemed by the sacrificial death of the effulgent hero and a new cosmogony, possible thanks to Love, the source of existence. Brünnhilde's final monologue, where Love is presented as the force that renews and transforms the world, is the logical conclusion of the idea of reunion with the true primordial foundations of life.

So, the tetralogy refracts Christian ideas in an indirect way. It is also possible to establish an inverse relationship. The legitimacy of interpreting the tetralogy in terms of the mystery of redemption (in the spirit of a profound reinterpretation of Christian ideas) is confirmed by Wagner's treatment of the image of Christ: the Christian Messiah appears as the central character in his sketches for the drama Jesus of Nazareth (1848). Jesus' sermons in this opus are very close to the moral views that Wagner expressed in the tetralogy[10] . The composer expressed his own vision of the radiant face of the Savior, without duplicating the canonical truths of the New Testament. The fundamental credo of Wagner's hero is to proclaim the eternal law of the spirit, which is love: "<..> if you act according to love," he says, "you will never sin" [21, p. 168]. [21, c. 168]. Turning to the Gospel motifs, Wagner gives them a new semantic connotation, as if illuminating them with his own ideas, which constantly excite him. For example, the Savior speaks of marriage, which is originally the result of the law of love. However, the composer emphasizes that this union is just if it is based on mutual feeling, but becomes oppressive when love is absent from it. Through the mouth of the Messiah, Wagner sets out his own thoughts on the subject: "The law says: 'Never commit adultery! And I say to you, do not marry without love. Marriage without love is dissolved at the moment when it is committed, and who entered into marriage without love, he has violated the law of matrimony " [21, c. 169]. This sermon is reminiscent of Wotan's reflections in the dialog with Frikka, where the head of the pantheon expressed his own judgment about the love of the Welsungs, which he does not regard as vicious at all: "What is sinful about their union, crowned with tender spring? Love's magic has ignited passion in them: is it possible to execute love?" (translated by V. Kolomiitsev). The motif of marriage and adultery outlines the moral views of R. Wagner himself, which remained unchanged throughout the composer's entire career. In the tetralogy, the musical drama Tristan und Isolde and the sketches for the drama Jesus of Nazareth, the composer does not conceive of true love in the light of immorality.

---

10 The original text of the sketches of Wagner's drama "Jesus of Nazareth", written on the motives of the Gospel hagiographies, is currently unavailable, but it can be judged by the cited quotations from this opus in the monograph by A. Lishtanberger [21, p. - 172]. Lishtanberger [21, pp. 167-172].

In his own reading of the New Testament, the composer corresponds to the law of property as one of the most immoral, since, in his view, every human being is equally entitled to look to nature as a source of satisfaction for his needs. However, nera venality flourishes in the human community, which accounts for the presence of temptation and sin in the world. In the sketches for the drama "Jesus of Nazareth" the composer outlined his own thoughts on this subject: "Whoever hoards wealth that can be stolen by thieves is the first to transgress the law, for he took from his neighbor what was necessary for the latter" [21, p. 170]. [21, c. 170]. Similarly, in "The Work of Future Art" Wagner writes about luxury, which "keeps the whole world in the iron chains of despotism" [8, p. 149] [8, p. 149], the same idea he consistently pursues in the tetralogy "The Ring of the Nibelung". The grandiose opera cycle is an embodiment of "the philosophy of history in sounds" [28, p. 9] [28, p. 9], but Wagner's reading of the Gospel story is equally historical, where the Savior's sermons are in tune with the social realities contemporary to the composer, revealing such plagues of the human community as greed, thirst for power and selfishness.

Let us summarize. The mystery of redemption in R. Wagner's tetralogy is revealed as a path of self-discovery of the main characters, refracted through the prism of Christian moral values, which paradoxically shine through the shell of pagan myth. The chosen analytical approach helps to reveal the dialogical synthesis of two closely interrelated models of worldview in R. Wagner's work - pagan and Christian. The comparison of the opera cycle with the sketches of the drama "Jesus of Nazareth" allows us to reveal the composer's constant moral attitudes, unchanged throughout the entire creative path of the master.

Conclusions

R. Wagner's religious and philosophical concept of Kunstreligion is connected with the embodiment of "Christian tragedy". R. Wagner's creativity is mystery-based. The idea of Kunstreligion in the context of R. Wagner's opera works appears as a worldview concept that was formed starting from The Flying Dutchman and ending with Parsifal, where it received a complete and concentrated expression in the stated genre of opera-mystery. Following the great initiates, R. Wagner proposes to search for God in himself (the unfinished drama "Jesus of Nazareth"), to comprehend the Truth not by means of rational and logical constructions, but by intuitive insight and mystical vision. The German composer's work invariably reveals the mystery-sterial threefold nature of history: 1) spiritual imperfection, the incompleteness of being; 2) inner torment, prompting the search for mystery Truth; 3) the achievement of transcendental harmony (Liebestod), conceived as perfection, infinity, universal dynamic statics - Love-Death. The search for Truth by R. Wagner's opera characters is defined by the mythologeme of the mystery Path, conceived as a process and a result (movement and a segment from the initial point to the final one). Liebestod is the outcome of the hero's mystery journey, his long-suffering acquisition of immortality through love and self-denial.

The idea of immortality, which defines the essence of the mysteries, appears to the author of the monograph as a "meaning clot" that synthesizes various heuristic "branches" in the cognitive activity of the German composer - Buddhism, Christianity, myth, philosophy, and fiction. The communicative space of Wagner's operas is a hermetic space where generally significant symbols and knowledge accumulated in various spheres of social consciousness are operated. Mythologems in R. Wagner's works acquire a unique meaning determined by the composer's worldview. R. Wagner's artistic consciousness acts as a communicative space, which communicates with the communicative space of world culture (semi- osphere). This process is connected with the composer's cognitive practice that forms the artistic consciousness of the German master. Thus, two communicative spaces interact: 1) R.

Wagner's artistic consciousness, which is based on the composer's thesaurus, his creative intellect (Wagner acts as a communicator and communicator), 2) the cultural and historical experience of mankind, which accumulates the stock of knowledge about the world (ontological ideas) accumulated in various spheres of social consciousness.

The three-membered nature of Wagner's fabulae is also connected with the idea of angelic service, which determines the motivation of the interactions of Wagner's characters in accordance with the mystery. The author of the monograph follows the theory of C. G. Jung, who represented Christian images as symbols reflecting the collective unconscious of mankind. The legitimacy of such an interpretation of Christian ideas in the works of R. Wagner is determined by his own understanding of the interaction between art and religion (the concept of Kun- streligion).

The archetype of the Angel is revealed in R. Wagner's work in various semantic readings. For example, through the prism of the idea of luminosity, which defines the nature of angels and their involvement with the Divine Light. The idea of luminosity is actualized in the musical and stage characteristics of the opera's characters - the angel maidens, the heavenly messenger Lohengrin and his beloved, the saintly simpleton and the sunny Siegfried the hero. In the introduction to the opera Lo- engrin, the lexeme of Divine Light is presented at the level of musical semantics. The final scenes of all of Wagner's operatic works, beginning with The Flying Dutchman and ending with Parsifal, are also imbued with light, expressing the idea of Liebestod at the intonation and dramaturgical level. An exception was The Meistersingers of Nuremberg, where the enlightened sound of the orchestra is associated with catharsis resulting from empathy with the opera characters, but the triumph of truth is shown outside the mystery idea. In R. Wagner's works, we find a mystery "graphic" - a transition from the world of sorrow to the sphere of transcendent world harmony. In his works, the German composer realizes the mystery of redemption, the ultimate goal of which is the acquisition of immortality in Love.

The angelic mission in the German composer's operas is carried out by spiritual mediators (lat. mediatrix) - angelic maidens (Senta, Elisabeth), God's messengers (Lohengrin, Parsifal), who together with the heroes-sinners realize the mystery of redemption. The spiritual path leads to redemption, interpreted by R. Wagner as a path of knowledge and self-knowledge. The tetralogy is no exception. The mystery of redemption in R. Wagner's grandiose opera cycle is connected with the mythologem of the Way; the idea of a life cycle that is closed and at the same time aspiring to eternity is realized in the work on micro- and macro-levels - love is eternal, it has a universal scale and is opposed to the singular as an embodiment of egoism; ontological milestones - birth, death, new cosmogony - together symbolize the idea of infinity on the ontological level. Myth interacts in the tetralogy with psychology, philosophy, including natural philosophy, and acute social motifs, forming a unique mix that determines the specificity of meaning-making in this unique work.

To conclude the study of the mysterious foundations of artistic consciousness and R. Wagner's work, I would like to conclude with the words of the author of the grandiose tetralogy concerning cognition: "From the moment when man felt his difference from nature and thus began to develop as a man, moving from the unconsciousness of natural animal existence to conscious life, when he thus opposed himself to nature and when the feeling of dependence on it gave impetus to the development of his thinking - from this moment delusion appeared as the first manifestation of consciousness. But delusion is the father of cognition, and the history of the development of cognition out of delusion is the history of the human race from the myths of the deep to the myths of the deep.

from antiquity to the present day" [8, p. 144]. [8, c. 144]. These words correspond in the best possible way to the concept of the famous tetralogy, at the same time responding to the mythologeme of the Path, which is a cross-cutting theme in the German master's work and determines the spiritual formation of the characters in the operas discussed in this monograph - the path from delusion (sinfulness) to the discovery of Truth (redemption).

Thus, the mystery beginning permeates R. Wagner's opera work, beginning with

"The Flying Dutchman" and ending with "Parsifal", affecting all textual levels: narrative and semantic, intonation and semantic, musical and dramaturgical.

List of references used

1. Author's program explanations to Wagner's opera overtures (trans. by T. G. Kovalyova) // Wagner R. Articles and materials / R. Wagner ; ed. by G. V. Krauklis, V. G. Gamrat-Kurek ; ed. by T. E. Tsitovich. G. V. Krauklis, V. G. Gamrat-Kurek ; ed. by T. E. Tsitovich. - Moscow : Music, 1974. - C. 55-62.

2. Anikst A. A. Comments on Goethe's "Faust" / A. A. Anikst // Selected Works: in 2 volumes / I. V. Goethe. - M., 1985. - VOL. 2. - P. 639-700.

3. Barthes R. Selected Works: Semiotics: Poetics; per. from Fr. G. K. Kosikov. / R. Bart. - Moscow: Progress, 1989. - 616 c.

4. Beketova N. The concept of transfiguration in Russian music / N. Beketova // Musical Culture of the Christian World: Proceedings of the International Scientific Conference. - Rostov-n/D: Publishing house of the Rostov State Conservatory named after S. S. Gubkin. C. V. Rakhmaninov, 2001. - C. 104-132.

5. Bondar S. V. Hymns of the Mother of God as "theology in sounds" (Orthodox tradition): thesis student. 5 course / scientific supervisor. L. V. Shapovalova; Kharkiv State Institute of Arts named after I. P. Kotlyarevsky, Department of Music Theory. - X., 2001. - 89 c.

6. Buddhist Treasures. Based on "The Treasure of Knowledge" by Jamgon Kongrtul Lodre Thaye BUDDDHISM TODAY, Vol.1, 1996, Kamtsang Choling USA: translated from Tib. by M. Golikov. Segers, Russian translation by S. Golikov [Electronic resource] - Access mode: kunpendelek.ru'library/buddhism/articles/treasure

7. Bhagavadgita: translation, introductory article and dictionary by B. L. Smirnov - Ashgabat: Ylym, 1978. [Electronic resource] - Access mode: yogalib.ru'veda- lit/545-bhagavatgita-smirnov

8. Wagner R. Selected works: transl. from German / R. Wagner; comp. and comment by I. A. Barsova, S. A. Osherov; intro. by A. F. Losev. A. F. Losev. - Moscow: Art, 1978. - 695 c.

9.   Wagner R. Selected articles / R. Wagner. - Moscow: Muzgiz, 1935. - 107 c.

10.   Wagner R. My life: in 2 vol. T. 1 / R. Wagner. - Moscow: Astrel, 2003. - 560 c. - (Memoirs).

11.   Wagner R. My life: in 2 vol. T. 2 / R. Wagner. - Moscow: Astrel, 2003. - 592 c. - (Memoirs).

12.   Wagner R. Letters. Diaries. Address to friends. T. 4. - The coming day / R. Wagner; ed. A. L. Volynsky, 1911. - 553 c.

13.   Vieru N. "Parsifal" - the result of Wagner's creative path // Richard Wagner: collection of articles. - M., 1987. - C. 191-222.

14.   Gorelik N. Abbot Gounod and his opera "Faust" / N. Gorelik // South-Russian Musical Almanac 2008 (5): a musical journal. - Rostov-n/D: Publishing house of the Rostov State Conservatory named after S. S. Gorelik. C. V. Rakhmaninov, 2009. - C. 74-82.

15.   Guliba A. Schelling. - 84 c. [Electronic resource] - Mode of access: www.rulit.me/books/shelling-read-48048-43.html

16.   Zhdanko A. The lexeme of light as a meaning-forming constant of N. A. Rimsky-Korsakov's musical theater / A. Zhdanko // Problems of interaction between art, pedagogy, theory and practice of ОСВІТU: А collection of scientific articles / Kharkiv State University of Arts and Sciences. I. P. Kotlyarevsky. - Kharyuv, 2005. - Vip. 22: Aspects of secondary musicology - II. - C. 143-151.

17.   Kaloshina G. Leonid Klinichev's opera diptych "Passion for Anna and Marina" / G. Kaloshina // South-Russian Musical Almanac 2015'3 (20). - Rostov-n/D: FGBOU VO "Rostov State Conservatoire named after S. S. Klinichev" / G. Kaloshina // South Russian Music Almanac 2015'3 (20). C. V. Rakhmaninov", 2015. - C. 75-83.

18.   Kaloshina G. Christian themes and problems of genre evolution of French opera and oratorio: from the origins to the XX century / G. Kaloshina // Musical Culture of the Christian World: Proceedings of the International Scientific Conference. - Rostov-n/D: Publishing House of the Rostov State Conservatory named after S. S.

Gubkin. C. V. Rakhmaninov, 2001. C. 297-316.

19.   Kaloshina G. Features of mystery in the religious and philosophical tragedies of Millau-Claudel // Problems of Musical Science 2010, № 1 (6): Russian scientific specialized journal; ed. by L. N. Shaimukhametova. Rostov n/D: Gilem, 2010. C. 137-142.

20.   The Book of Angels: Anthology of Christian Angelology / edited by D. Y. Dorofeev. - SPb.: Amfora. TID Amfora, 2005. - 553 c.

21.   Lishtanberge A. Richard Wagner as a poet and thinker: per. from Fr. / A. Lishtanberge. - Moscow: Algorithm, 1997. - 477 c.

22.   Losev A. F. F. The historical meaning of Richard Wagner's aesthetic outlook / A. F. Losev // R. Wagner. Selected Works. - Moscow: Art, 1978. - C. 7-48.

23.   Losev A. F. F. Richard Wagner's problem in the past and present: (In connection with the analysis of his tetralogy "The Ring of the Nibelung") / A. F. Losev // Voprosy aesthetiki. - M., 1968. - Vyp. 8. - C. 67-196.

24.   Lotman Yu. M. Selected articles: in 3 vol. Vol. I: Articles on semiotics and topology of culture / Y. M. Lotman. - Tallinn: Alexandra, 1992. - 247 c.

25.   Mann T. The Suffering and Greatness of Richard Wagner / T. Mann // Collected Works: in 10 vol. - M., 1961. - T. 10: Articles 1929 - 1955. - C. 102-174.

26.   Mikhailova O.. S. Biblical legend in Italian opera of the first half of the XIX century ("Moses" by J. Rossini, "Nebuchadnezzar" by J. Verdi): Cand. Cand. of Art History: 17.00.02 / O. S. Mikhailova. - Rostov-n/D, 2014. - 182 c.

27.   Musical Culture of the Christian World: Materials of the International Scientific Conference. - Rostov-n/D: Publishing house of the Rostov State Conservatory named after S. S. S. Gorky. C. V. Rakhmaninov, 2001. - 500 c.

28.   Musical aesthetics of nineteenth-century Germany: in 2 vols. T. 1 / comp. A. Mikhailov, V. Shestakov; ed. by N. Shakhnazarov. - Moscow: Music, 1981. - 415 p., notes. - (Monuments of musical and aesthetic thought).

29. Naukovyi BÌCHUK: zb. nauk. pr. za mater. mižnar. nauk. conf. / National Mus. akad. Ukraina ìM. P. I. Tchaikovsky. - K., 1999. - Vip. 4: Music i Bible. - 248 c.

30. Naumova E. A. Richard Wagner's Mystery Theater: "Parsifal" and its sacred dramaturgy: dissertation ... ... Cand. of Art History: 17. 00. 01 / E. A. Naumova. - K., 2006. - 180 c.

31. Plato. Selected dialogues / Plato. - Moscow: Khud. literature, 1963. - 441 c.

32. Rudnev, V. Encyclopedic dictionary of culture of the XX century / V. Rudnev. - Moscow: Agraf, 2001. - 608 c.

33. Sadovnikova E. "The Tale of the Invisible City of Kitizh and the Maiden Fevronia" by N. A. Rimsky-Kosakov in the light of the problem of iconicity / E. Sadovnikova // Problems of interdemocracy of art, pedagogy, theory and practice of education: a collection of scientific papers / Kharkiv State University of Arts and Sciences. I. P. Kotlyarevsky. - Kharyuv, 2009. - Vip. 26: Aspects of secondary musicology - III. Vivere est cogitare. - C. 35-51.

34. Svasyan K. A. Philosophical outlook of Goethe / K. A. Svasyan. - Yerevan: Armenian Academy of Sciences. SSR, 1983 - 183 p.

35. Dictionary of Antiquity / ed. by V. I. Kuzishchin - Moscow: Progress 1989. I. Kuzishchin - M.: Progress, 1989. - 704 c.

36. Tyshko S. V. V. The image of the Light of Tabor and the processes of style formation in the operas of M. Mussorgsky / S. V. Tyshko // Musical Culture of the Christian World: Proceedings of the International Scientific Conference. - Rostov-n/D: Publishing House of the Rostov State Conservatory named after S. V. Tyshko // Music Culture of the Christian World: Proceedings of the International Scientific Conference. C. V. Rakhmaninov, 2001. - C. 422-435.

37. Upanishads / translation and foreword by A. Y. Syrkin - M.: Nauka, 1967. [Electronic resource   ].   -   Mode of access :
psylib.ukrweb.net/books/upani01/index.htm

38. Hübner K. The truth of myth / K. Hübner. - Moscow: Respublika, 1996. - 448 с.

39. Cherkashina M. Evangelical motifs in the works of R. Wagner // Naukovyi ВÌCHUK: zb. nauk. pr. za mater. mižnar. nauk. conf. / National Academy of Music. Ukraina ìм. P. I. Tchaikovsky. - K., 1999. - Vip. 4: Music i Bible. - С. 159-166.

40. Shalagshov B. B. "Faust" by J. V. Goethe and the problem of the spiritual essence of man in the Schmeckian literature at the turn of the 18th-19th centuries. Goethe's Faust and the problem of spiritual essence of people in Schmeckian literature at the turn of the 18th-19th centuries: author's thesis .... D. in Philology: 10.01.04 / B. B. Shalagshov. - K., 2003. - 40 с.

41. Steiner R. Mysteries of antiquity and Christianity [Electronic resource] / R. Steiner. - Mode of access:

http://moshkow.library.kr.ua/cgibin/htmlKOI.pl/URIKOVA/STEINER/misterii .txt

42. Shyure E. The great initiated. [Electronic resource] / E. Shyure. - Mode of access: http://fortune.hop.ru/txts/dopolnit_ogl.htm

43. Jung, K. G. Archetype and Symbol / K. G. Jung; comp. and intro. by A. M. Rutkevich. A. M. Rutkevich. - Moscow: Renaissance, 1991. - 304 с.

44. Jung K. G. Collected Works. Answer to Job: transl. / K. G. Jung - M.: Canon + ROOI "Rehabilitation, 2006. - 352 с. - (History of psychology in monuments).

45. Borchmeyer D. Die Festspielidee im Spannungsfeld von Hofkultur und "Kunst-religion". Goethe - Richard Wagner - Ludwig II / D. Borchmeyer // Bayreuther Festspielbuches.- 2001 - P. 18-25.

46. Eger M. Die Bibliotheken des Richard-Wagner-Museums und der Richard-Wagner-Gedenktstatte. / M. Eger // Archival materials of the Kharkov Wagner Society. - [Manuscript].

47. Kienzle U. Venus - Maria - Elisabeth. Wagners weibliche Dreifaltigkeit in Tannhause // Bayreuther Festspielbuches. - 2003 - P. 66-77.

48. Müller U. Vom Lauf der Welt / U. Müller, O. Panagl // Bayreuther Festspielbu-

ches. - 2007. - P. 100-115.

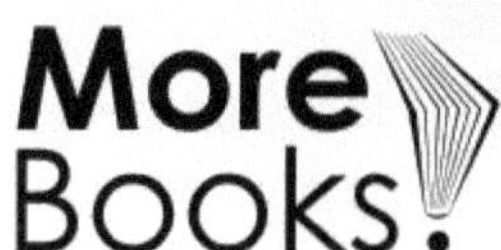

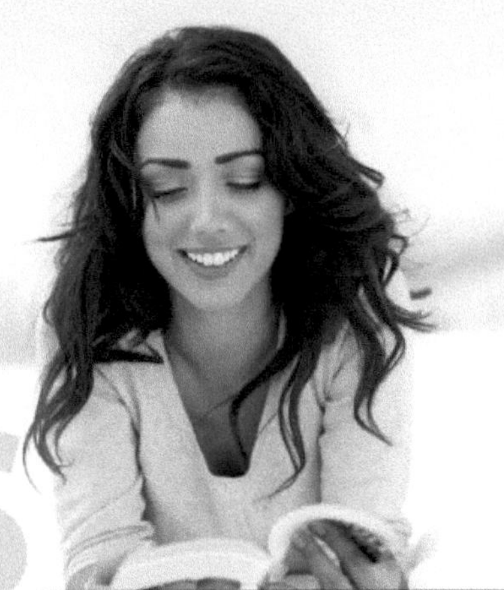

Buy your books fast and straightforward online - at one of world's fastest growing online book stores! Environmentally sound due to Print-on-Demand technologies.

Buy your books online at
www.morebooks.shop

Kaufen Sie Ihre Bücher schnell und unkompliziert online – auf einer der am schnellsten wachsenden Buchhandelsplattformen weltweit! Dank Print-On-Demand umwelt- und ressourcenschonend produziert.

Bücher schneller online kaufen
www.morebooks.shop

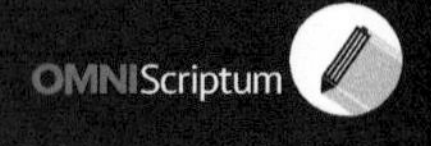

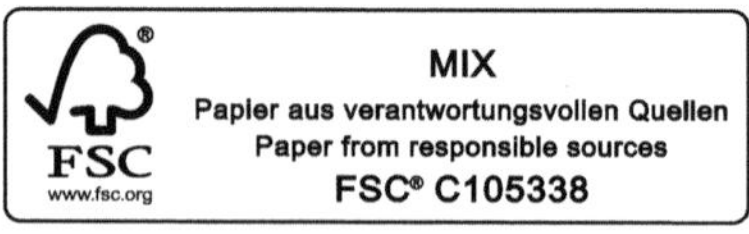